Female *Othello*s

İnci Bilgin Tekin

Female *Othello*s

PETER LANG

Bibliographic Information published by the Deutsche Nationalbibliothek
The Deutsche Nationalbibliothek lists this publication in the Deutsche Nationalbibliografie; detailed bibliographic data is available in the internet at http://dnb.d-nb.de.

Library of Congress Cataloging-in-Publication Data
A CIP catalog record for this book has been applied for at the Library of Congress.

ISBN 978-3-631-74869-5 (Print)
E-ISBN 978-3-631-75726-0 (E-PDF)
E-ISBN 978-3-631-75727-7 (EPUB)
E-ISBN 978-3-631-75728-4 (MOBI)
DOI 10.3726/b14184

© Peter Lang GmbH
Internationaler Verlag der Wissenschaften
Berlin 2018
All rights reserved.

Peter Lang – Berlin · Bern · Bruxelles · New York · Oxford · Warszawa · Wien

This publication has been peer reviewed.

www.peterlang.com

Contents

In tribute to my dear "Shakespeare" lecturer
Ercüment ATABAY whom we lost this winter.

Acknowledgements

This book is primarily inspired by an undergraduate course titled "Adaptations and Rewrites in Contemporary Drama," which I taught to Boğaziçi University (BU) Translation Studies students between 2010 and 2012 in İstanbul, Turkey. Coming from a purely literature background, this course enabled me to realize how the two concepts "adaptation" and "rewrite" are received differently in the two disciplines as well as in performance. A considerable part of this study was conducted during my one-year-long postdoctoral research carried out at De Montfort University's Center for Adaptations in Leicester, UK, which provided me with an active research environment that included various lectures, seminars, conferences and workshops on adaptation theory, as well as a rich library. The library research conducted at the University of Birmingham's Institute of Shakespeare in Stratford-upon-Avon has also greatly contributed to my literature survey. The undergraduate elective course titled "Contemporary Adaptations and Appropriations of Shakespearean Tragedies," which I taught to BU Western Languages and Literature students, and the graduate course titled "Intertextual Relations," which I taught to İstanbul University (IU) American Literature students in fall 2014 and spring 2015, also contributed to this study, feeding my perspective through various discussions. *Restaging 'Othello': Contemporary Women Playwrights* also benefited from a six weeks' research affiliation at the University of Leicester's School of English. This study is supported by Boğazici University research project titled "Rewriting Shakespeare in Contemporary Intercultural Context." (BAP project coded 15L00P1)

I owe my deepest gratitude to my dear drama teachers Aslı Tekinay and Özden Sözalan for making it all possible with their everlasting support. My heartfelt thanks go to Professor Aslı Tekinay for inspiring my "Contemporary Adaptations of Shakespeare" project with her invaluable recommendations, speedy feedbacks and great enthusiasm. I feel deeply indebted to my graduate thesis supervisor Professor Özden Sözalan whose expertise on dramaturgy and innovative perspectives I consulted at each and every stage of this project.

I would like to thank Professor Nursel İçöz whose very intriguing "Intergeneric and Interdisciplinary Relations" graduate course syllabus shaped most of the theoretical discussions in this study. Many thanks to Professor Cevza Sevgen for her incredible support during the literature survey. I would also like to thank Professor Suat Karantay and Professor Şehnaz Tahir Gürçağlar whose guidance and suggestions provided an interdisciplinary perspective on Adaptation Studies and Translation Studies.

I am indebted to Professor Deborah Cartmell and Dr. Emma Parker who hosted me in Leicester, De Montfort University Center for Adaptations and University of Leicester Department of English, respectively, offering many privileges and a friendly atmosphere in which to work. I owe a sincere gratitude to Professor Zeynep Naz Atay, the Director of BU School of Foreign Languages, for being very cooperative and supportive throughout the research project. I would also like to thank my dear colleagues at BU Advanced English Unit for their enormous support and understanding throughout this study. Many thanks to all my students at BU and IU for opening new horizons with vivid discussions.

Last but not least, my sincere thanks go to members of my family, my loving son Mert Tekin and my very supportive husband Dr. Bülent Tekin, who together accompanied me during my postdoctoral research in the UK, as well as my newborn baby Derin Tekin for her patience during the proofreading process. Many thanks to my dear sister Güller Pınar Bilgin who by now is also my colleague and my dear parents Professor Leman Bilgin and Servet Bilgin, whose academic enthusiasm and work ethics guided my studies.

In memories of my grandparents and my father-in-law...

Introduction

Introducing the contemporary perceptions of *Othello*, an ever controversial play for postcolonial and feminist readers, this study is the first book which specifically focuses on adaptations of *Othello*. With its conventional female representation in a considerably patriarchal context, *Othello* has inevitably initiated contemporary women playwrights' projects of rewriting the canonical play. It is noteworthy that between 1979 and 2011, four stage adaptations of the play were introduced by contemporary women American and Canadian playwrights: Paula Vogel's *Desdemona: A Play About a Handkerchief* (1979), Ann-Marie MacDonald's *Goodnight Desdemona, Good Morning Juliet* (1988), Djanet Sears's *Harlem Duet* (2002) and Toni Morrison's *Desdemona.* (2011) These transformative plays freely adapt *Othello* into their distinct understandings of feminism. While Vogel and MacDonald's plays reveal a lesbian feminist concern, Sears and Morrison's texts reflect the feminism of women of color. Their different understandings of feminism also shape the adaptive discourse and adaptive strategies which are noteworthy in categorizing these plays as "free or loose adaptations," "appropriations" or "revisions."

It should be noted that the four contemporary women playwrights commonly come from intellectual backgrounds and are all responsive readers of Shakespeare. The Canadian lesbian feminist writer and journalist Ann-Marie MacDonald has a BA in Theater. She notes that she was influenced by LGBT's activism and that she followed the second feminist wave closely. Currently Ann-Marie MacDonald and her partner Alisa Parmer, a theater director, have been working on an adaptation of *Hamlet* for Stratford festival. MacDonald's writing primarily reflects her feminist ideology which broadly reacts to any type of oppression. She was highly praised for her first published creative work *Good Night Desdemona, Good Morning Juliet.* MacDonald's attitude towards Shakespeare, in her only published adaptation of Shakespeare so far, can be considered as a mock serious one, showing the major characteristics of a postmodern parody.

Djanet Sears, similarly, comes from a Canadian background, with a BA in Theater. Sears teaches drama both at the University of Toronto and at the University College in Toronto. Sears's stage play African Solo was recognized as the first stage play to be written by a Canadian woman of African descent and was followed by her other two major works, *Harlem Duet* and *The Adventures of a Black Girl in Search of God*. Sears is praised for her inclusion of West-African traditions in her plays. In content, she usually addresses the issues of race and gender. Sears's dialogue with the Bard implies political activism, offering a specific focus on black rights and black women's oppression.

Paula Vogel is an American professor of theater and a lesbian feminist activist who was the 1998 winner of the Pulitzer Prize in Drama. Vogel's creative work usually addresses social issues such as sexual abuse and prostitution. *Desdemona: A Play About a Handkerchief* is her second most well-known work, following *How I Learned to Drive*. Vogel's adaptive strategy in revisiting *Othello* with a female focus can be related to her background as an academic and her candidacy for canonization as a Pulitzer awarded writer.

As for Toni Morrison, the well-known American writer and professor, she comes from literature background. Racial issues and female oppression have always been on Morrison's agenda, and she was praised for her distinct style in addressing such tense issues. Many of her novels, especially *Beloved, Bluest Eye, Sula,* are usually included in the curriculums of literature departments worldwide. Her only published short story "Recitatif," which was anthologized in *Norton Anthology of American Literature*, has also recently been at the center of scholarly interest.

The purpose of this book is to examine the contemporary stage adaptations of *Othello* by the four noteworthy contemporary playwrights, while discussing their plays both within and outside the framework of Adaptation Studies. Drawing on postcolonial and feminist theories along with psychoanalytical theories and theories of adaptation, this book explores the adaptive levels, contexts and strategies of the four women playwrights in revising *Othello*.

It is one of the most remarkable characteristics of *Othello* that it is a play lending itself to adaptations. The story of Othello, which draws on the Italian writer Cinthio's text *Un Capitano Moro*, has always had an adaptive potential. Shakespeare himself revised the play between the 1622 Quarto and the 1623 Folio. *Othello* has been initially appropriated by Maurice Dowling for stage as *Othello Travestie* (1839). In addition to directors who were quite loyal to Shakespeare's text in their staging of the play such as many Royal Shakespeare Company's directors, two prominent directors, the American theater director and playwright Charles Marowitz and the Canadian writer Ken Mitchell, loosely adapted *Othello* for stage in the 1970s. While Marowitz challenges the racist context of *Othello* in *An Othello*, which takes place in the States, Mitchell's *Cruel Tears* revisits *Othello* in a rural context.

Othello has also aroused considerable interest in cinema, the earliest film adaptation dating back to 1909, the silent film era. Offering a detailed analysis of Orson Welles's *Othello* (1952), the film critic Lorne M. Buchman notes: "Othello has received the least critical attention and continues to be one of the most rarely seen of all cinematic adaptations of the plays." (53) *Othello* has not received much interest as compared to a number of its stage adaptations, either. However, the three innovative contemporary screen adaptations of the play, Oliver Parker's *Othello* (1995) in which Laurence Fishburne appears as the first black actor playing Othello on a major screen project, O (2001) which loosely adapts Othello into an American high school context and Vishal Bhardwaj's Indian *Othello* titled *Omkara* (2006) which is a very good example of an intercultural transfer, should be noted as exceptions.

As Thomas Cartelli notes, *Othello* has been marked by many contemporary literary scholars as one of the most interesting tragedies by Shakespeare, since it accommodates the potential for both feminist and postcolonial readings with its representation of a discriminatory society. (24) However, the debate on whether Shakespeare himself was sexist and colonialist himself should be abandoned within the scope of this study for two different reasons. The first reason is that this study deals with associations with or receptions of Shakespeare more than it deals with William Shakespeare as a person. Another noteworthy reason is that this study specifically focuses on *Othello*, a more revolutionary tragedy by Shakespeare compared to its contemporaries, due to its representation of a black character as its protagonist. Drawing on Catherine Silverstone's argument "[...] no matter how the character is cast, the body of Othello is racially marked." (78), one can read Shakespeare's representation of Othello's dark body as his problematization of the existing racial context which stereotypes and oppresses the black subjects. Representing Othello as his dark and powerful protagonist in juxtaposition with the white racist Iago as his antagonist, Shakespeare foregrounds the racist context parallel to Othello's fatal error, his "hamartia" in the Aristotelian context, male jealousy.

As Karen Newman suggests, contemporary readers should read Shakespeare resistant to patriarchal and colonial discourses implied in the plays, while at the same time searching for alternative modes of representation, revising these contexts. (219–220). In other words, Shakespeare's *Othello* is very brave and remarkably challenging as an early 17th-century English attempt to represent both the black subject as a protagonist and a white aristocratic woman in a marital relation with him. It is crucial to note that *Othello*, therefore, is a play "revis[ing]" a predating short story, *Un Capitano Moro*, by the 16th-century Italian writer Cinthio (Giovanni Battista Giraldi), dramatizing its contents of 'racism' and 'female victimization'. In this respect, in the form of an intergeneric rewrite, Shakespeare builds on Cinthio's question of chastity within the European margins of conformity and dignity, proving its disfunctionality and offering further room for criticism.

In this study, the term 're-vision' is used as an adaptive strategy for a feminist and/or postcolonial reconstruction, drawing on both Adrienne Rich's feminist understanding of the term as an intention to "critical[ly]" explore the previous traditions of writing "not to pass a tradition but to break its hold over us [women]" (70), and the black critic Henri Louis Gates's notion of "signify[ing] on" which he defines as to "revise" and to "alter" as a means of postcolonial resistance through remembering and changing. While Rich's feminist perspective makes a call for women writers to "revise the old texts" and thus "write ourselves [the female presence] back into the history" (69), Henri Louis Gates offers a black semiotic model which traces the roots of black tradition of writing to the black vernacular, signifying monkey and reads it also as a response to the Eurocentric tradition of writing. (XX–XV) Given this context, the term "re-vision" signals a feminist and/or postcolonial context, rewriting the earlier text from a liberating perspective.

Accommodating an addressed intertextual dialogue with its source text in an intergeneric or interdisciplinary form, adaptation is closely linked to translation and performance, especially given the case of stage adaptations. According to many translation studies, scholars including Susan Bassnet, Patrice Pavis and Andre Lefevere, translating a dramatic text is different than other acts of translation since drama is a performative and therefore an innately adaptive genre. (Bassnet 90, Pavis 5–15) After the 1960s' shift in the focus of translation studies from a source-centered approach to a target-centered understanding, translation was redefined as a type of rewrite, inevitably "manipulat[ive]" in its relation to the canon, reflecting certain ideological choices. (Lefevere 2) However in literary studies, rewrite is considered as a type of adaptation which is more revolutionary in its relation to the inspiring text. As for film scholars, the term adaptation implies literature to film transfer while given the context of dramaturgy, it signifies a text to stage transfer, both of which can own either a loyal or free adaptive perspective and/or introduce a cross-cultural context. In this respect, the term "adaptation" can be taken as a targeted intertextual, intergeneric and interdisciplinary process which draws on the intercultural encounter of the source text and its adapted version.

The history of adaptations can be traced to 1st century A.D. when the Roman philosopher, dramatist and humorist, Seneca offers his own versions of *Medea*, *Oedipus* and *Agamemnon*, plays associated with his predecessors Euripides, Sophocles and Aeschylus, respectively. Although classical parody is usually identified with a satirical perspective, the first genre that accommodates adaptive qualities may be considered as classical parody, dating back to Aristotelian times. Parody is a recurrent style in different times and traditions of literature, from Aristophanes of the classical Greek to Geoffrey Chaucer of the Medieval English, from Cervantes of 17th century Spain to Henry Fielding of 18th century England. 'Imitation' or 'inspiration' can be noted among the most recurrent terms in early theoretical works by Plato, Horace and Longinus, being gradually shaped into our contemporary consciousness. While in 1598 Ben Johnson links the term "parody" to "absurdity," John Dryden offers a definition which is closer to its contemporary understanding as "making fun of" and "re-creating" the given context. Classical parody has been gradually transformed into our contemporary times in the form of postmodern parody.

In her comprehensive work *A Theory of Parody*, Linda Hutcheon argues that postmodern parody replaces the satirical perspective of the classical parody through "repetition with a critical distance." (32) As Hutcheon acknowledges writing her later work *A Theory of Adaptations*, there is a close link between parody and adaptation. Ever since the 1970s, when adaptation studies was first introduced as a new academic field building on interdisciplinary approaches, the major debate among the adaptation studies scholars has always centered on the issue of fidelity in adaptations. Parallel to both post-1960s transformation of translation studies from a source-text-oriented approach to a target-text-oriented one and the ground-breaking suggestion that reader-centered criticism should replace author-centered perspectives (late 1960s), adaptation studies has also developed the notion of "free" or "loose" adaptations, which are used synonymously, drawing on the level of omissions from and additions to the source text.

In her seminal work *A Theory of Adaptation*, Linda Hutcheon offers the following definition of "adaptation" in its broadest sense:

- An acknowledged transposition of a recognizable other work or work
- A creative act and an interpretive act of appropriation/salvaging
- An extended intertextual engagement with the adapted work (8)

Hutcheon's inclusive definition treats both loose or free and loyal adaptations as "adaptations," while it underlines three different modes of adaptation, drawing on their direct or indirect relationships with the source text. It is also noteworthy that unlike other Adaptation Studies theorists, Hutcheon neglects to use the recently popularized term "appropriation."

Mark Fortier and Daniel Fischlin, specifically, define "appropriation" as "a hostile take-over, a seizure of authority over the original" in a political context (3) while Julie Sanders considers it as "a decisive journey away from the informing source into a wholly new cultural product and domain." (26) As Julie Sanders notes, adaptation usually offers "a commentary on the source text," "from a revising point of view from the 'original.'" (18, 19) In this respect, appropriation functions more politically, as a more subversive mode within adaptations, which in turn distinguishes appropriation from loose or free adaptations. Drawing on the given definitions, "adaptation" is considered an addressed and extended intertextual and/or intergeneric dialogue and "appropriation" is taken as a more deconstructive mode of adaptation, challenging the authority of the source text and its writer in the canon, usually to indicate an ideological stance. To be more specific, while the terms "adaptation" and "rewrite" are used both interchangeably and in a broad sense to accommodate both loyal and loose/free adaptations and/or intergeneric/interdisciplinary rewrites, the terms "re-vision" and "appropriation" are used, respectively, in the sense of reconstructive and deconstructive adaptations.

When it is adaptations of a canonical name as Shakespeare, the fidelity debate of whether to show gratitude or departure from the source text and its writer becomes even more explicit. Michael Dobson notes that "Shakespeare has been as normatively constitutive of British national identity as the drinking of afternoon tea." (7) Having been perceived as a national signifier, Shakespeare has usually been adapted and rarely appropriated in the UK. Tom Stoppard's *Rosencrantz and Guildenstern Are Dead* (1966) and Edward Bond's *Lear* (1971) can be considered among the loosest adaptations of Shakespeare in the UK, due to the number of additions and omissions to/from their source texts. While Stoppard offers an existentialist rewrite of *Hamlet* in the form of a tragicomedy, the socialist writer Bond rewrites *King Lear* in the form of epic, to offer a social critique. However, neither of the plays problematizes what Shakespeare and his plays signify but rather provide political interpretations of the two plays' representations of hierarchy and autocracy. As for Shakespeare in the States, Michael D. Bristol acknowledges that "Shakespeare has been recognized as an institution in America" (203) while the name signifies "resistence to coercive authority" (204) at the same time. As Walter Cohen argues, while Marxist criticism is more influential in post 1980 Shakespeare studies in UK, American scholars of Shakespeare reflect their "national and geographical distance from Shakespeare" (21) onto their new historicist and feminist perspectives on Shakespeare. (19) The fact that many appropriations of Shakespeare's works originate from the States supports these theories. As for the Canadian receptions of Shakespeare, which in turn can be taken as signifiers of Canada's "ambivalent identity" (Fortier 342), they define themselves through both continuity and difference from the European origin. This stance reflects on the Canadian adaptations of Shakespeare explicitly, situating their adaptations in between the British and American motivations of revisiting and reimagining.

It is now accepted by many literature authorities that the word Shakespeare no longer means the writer and his texts but implies a whole canon of literature. While being revisited by contemporary writers and critics, William Shakespeare is often depersonalized and "virtual"[ized] (Fischlin and Fortier 17), having become a signifier for the canon as well as a noteworthy reference for past and present modes and codes of representation. In other words, adapting Shakespeare inevitably signifies both an easy access to the heart of canonical issues or theoretical discussions on the one hand and a considerable writerly challenge for a potentially canonical writer. The idea of adapting Shakespeare inevitably raises questions of authority or authorship. Shakespeare has been frequently revisited in mainstream and less-known projects of drama and narrative besides cinema and music. While a group of adaptors respond to Shakespeare loyally to show their indebtedness as his enthusiastic readers, some adaptors, in rivalry, foreground their authorial debate with Shakespeare.

While examining different levels of adaptations and various adaptive strategies in four contemporary Othellos, the notions of canonization and authority will be addressed. Paula Vogel, Ann-Marie MacDonald, Djanet Sears and Toni Morrison's feminist and postcolonial readings of or responses to Shakespeare's *Othello* will be examined from a comparative and contrastive perspective. In her preface to the groundbreaking collection of essays *Playing in the Dark*, Toni Morrison suggests that "Writing and reading are not all that distinct for a writer" and underlines the significance of "response-ability" in both. (XIII) As contemporary women playwrights loosely adapt *Othello* into contemporary, postmodern, American, Canadian, postcolonial or feminist contexts, they not only present themselves as contemporary readers or audiences of Shakespeare but also as new writers searching for their own places within the literary canon, in response to *Othello*. In this respect, the following lines by Linda Hutcheon are very noteworthy, "Adaptations of Shakespeare, in particular, may be intended as tributes, or as a way to supplant canonical cultural authority," (93) since the four appropriations of *Othello* incorporate the two motivations of a readerly enthusiasm and a writerly ambition or a gender/race conscious reading and a postcolonial/feminist rewrite. This understanding, in turn, relocates *Othello* as both Shakespeare's and not Shakespeare's. Given this context, this study considerably benefits from psychoanalytical theories on "anxiety" and "influence" or "authorial" struggle for authority.

The four women playwrights addressed in this book bring into *Othello* a contemporary perspective of the reader and/or the literary critic, which is reflected on either the content or the form of their writing. For instance, Ann-Marie MacDonald's heroine Constance, a young and enthusiastic academic, finds herself among the characters of *Othello* and *Romeo and Juliet*, with the consciousness of both plots. While Constance tries to break the tragic cycle with deliberate involvement in the plot, the text is transformed into a tragicomedy as well as a postmodern parody when her contemporary perspective is added. Similarly, Djanet Sears's innovative black heroine Billie has Shakespeare's books in her shared library with Othello while Othello and Yago (Sears's Iago) are depicted as academic rivals in the department of English. Sears's representation of her characters, with contemporary consciousness, as readers and critics of Shakespeare, also reinforces the choice of adaptation, which is a self-reflexive and intertextual form of writing. As for Paula Vogel's *Desdemona: A Play About a Handkerchief*, the contemporary intellectuals' questioning of whether ethics is a collective or individual issue, is foregrounded. Moreover, Vogel's contemporary consciousness addresses the major concern of the play as that of the handkerchief, which is both reflected on the subject matter and the adaptive strategy. Similarly, Toni Morrison's *Desdemona* adds a distinctly contemporary and highly intellectual perspective into the play by representing the characters in an after-life, giving a moral account of the earlier events. Morrison's adaptive choice of writing a postquel to *Othello* reflects the contemporary readerly perspective.

The adaptive discourses and the adaptive strategies are explicitly what distinguishes the four adaptations. While Ann-Marie MacDonald and Paula Vogel's plays question *Othello*'s representation of gender stereotypes and female sexuality in a parodic way, Djanet Sears' and Toni Morrison's calls for rethinking *Othello*'s representation of Africa and the black subject, from the viewpoints of two black female characters, is very serious in tone. Ann-Marie MacDonald juxtaposes the two tragedies of *Othello* and *Romeo and Juliet* with specific focuses on Desdemona and Juliet. Paula Vogel dethrones Othello and reduces *Othello* into two acts by centralizing Desdemona, Emilia and Bianca and plotting her play around the issue of handkerchief. Djanet Sears writes a precursor to *Othello*, centralizing her alternative black female character, Billie, who is Othello's ex-girlfriend. Toni Morrison writes a postquel to *Othello*, representing the characters in after-life and giving life to Desdemona's black maid Barbary, who had taught her the willow's song.

Although most feminist criticism identifies *Hamlet* with misogyny, there are few stage adaptations of *Hamlet* by women writers. It is therefore striking that *Othello*, a play usually associated with the issue of race, is the most reworked tragedy by Shakespeare even when given the context of contemporary women writers adapting Shakespeare. In this respect, this study seeks answers to the following questions: 1) Why are the four contemporary women playwrights interested in adapting *Othello* rather than any other plays by Shakespeare? 2) Do their adaptations of *Othello* adapt *Othello*, the play, or rather rewrite Othello, the protagonist? 3) How far do these playwrights depart from the source text as they adapt *Othello* into their target cultures? 4) In what ways do their adaptations respond to contemporary theories such as feminism, postcolonialism and poststructuralism? 5) What kinds of writerly dialogues with Shakespeare are observed in the rewriting process?

Seeking these answers, this book examines four contemporary stage adaptations of *Othello* by noteworthy women playwrights, namely Ann-Marie MacDonald, Paula Vogel, Djanet Sears and Toni Morrison, while discussing their plays both within and outside the framework of Adaptation Studies. A comparative and analytical perspective is owned in reading the adaptations in relation to the source text and other adaptations while an interdisciplinary scope is targeted in treating 'adaptation' as a genre at the crossroads between literature, performance and translation.

Drawing on the biographical sources and interviews, one should note that coming from intellectual and/or academic backgrounds, the four playwrights are enthusiastic readers of Shakespeare. For instance, the 1998 Pulitzer Prize winner playwright Paula Vogel is an American feminist theorist and a university Professor. Her 1979 adaptation of *Othello* titled *Desdemona: A Play About a Handkerchief* is a free adaptation offering a prequel to Shakespeare's tragedy. The recipient of several national awards, Canadian playwright Ann-Marie MacDonald has a BA degree in Theater. In 1988, she published her celebrated play *Goodnight Desdemona, Good Morning Juliet*, which loosely adapts the two major tragedies by Shakespeare, *Othello* and *Romeo and Juliet*. Similar to MacDonald, the black Canadian playwright and Drama Professor Djanet Sears was awarded Canada's highest literary award, The Governor's General Literary Award. Published in 2002, her play *Harlem Duet* is usually considered as a precursor to *Othello*. The 1988 Pulitzer Prize winning American novelist and essayist Toni Morrison is also a Professor of Literature. Morrison's works have been included in many literature course syllabi. In her second play *Desdemona*, published in 2012, Morrison offers a free adaptation of *Othello*.

Canadian feminist playwright Ann-Marie MacDonald's *Goodnight Desdemona, Good Morning Juliet* and American feminist dramatist Paula Vogel's *Desdemona: A Play About A Handkerchief* are feminist adaptations of *Othello*. In this respect, feminist theorists, including Julia Kristeva and Adrienne Rich, are revisited as well as the theorists of Adaptation Studies. Canadian playwright Djanet Sears's *Harlem Duet* and American writer Toni Morrison's *Desdemona*, which also accommodate feminist themes, are read as black cultural adaptations. Therefore, women of color feminism is incorporated into the analysis, with references to third wave theorists including bell hooks, Barbara Smith, Gayatri C. Spivak and Gloria Anzaldua, in order to explain double oppression women of color have been exposed to. To better explore the postcolonial context, references to Henri Louis Gates's notion of "signifying upon," Edward Said's understanding of "orientalism" and Homi K. Bhabha's conception of "hybridity," are also included. The distinctive American and Canadian, lesbian and heterosexual, white and black qualities of the plays are examined within the cultural contexts these new Othellos highlight. Biographical information on these contemporary women playwrights, most of which come from intellectual or academic backgrounds, is also related to their dialogues with a canonical name as Shakespeare. The authorial aspect is discussed in Chapter 4, which, following a comparative method, offers a psychoanalytical perspective on the adaptive strategies of Vogel, MacDonald, Sears and Morrison.

This study provides an interdisciplinary perspective on adaptation while it follows a comparative approach by analyzing the adaptations in relation to the source text and one another, as it is now an established knowledge in Adaptation Studies that adaptations of Shakespeare usually draw on one another. Chapter 1 offers a theoretical perspective in addressing the concepts adaptation, appropriation, revision, rewrite as well as in discussing the canonical significance of Shakespeare and adaptations of Shakespeare, parallel to the rise of Adaptation Studies. Chapter 2 analyzes the Canadian playwright Ann-Marie MacDonald's and the American playwright Paula Vogel's appropriations of Shakespeare's source text, Othello, in relation to lesbian feminist contexts as well as Canadian and American backgrounds their plays introduce. Chapter 3 focuses on the Canadian playwright Djanet Sears and the American writer Toni Morrison's appropriations of Othello in terms of their suggestive black feminist perspectives as well as the

21

underlying Canadian and American contexts. Chapters 2 and 3 also discuss the adaptive strategies these playwrights follow in appropriating a canonical text like *Othello*, from a comparative perspective. Conclusion offers a comparative analysis of the four contemporary writers' intertextual dialogues with the Bard, in relation to the contemporary issues of authorship and authority.

Inspired in 2016 as a tribute right after the 400th anniversary of the Great Bard's death, this study celebrates the canonical adaptor and the ever-adapted Shakespeare as a signifier of the adaptive process itself. It is anticipated that this study will contribute to studies on Adapting Shakespeare as well as projects on contemporary women playwrights in being the first book to specifically examine stage adaptations of *Othello* and the first study to cover Ann-Marie MacDonald, Djanet Sears, Paula Vogel and Toni Morrison together.

1 A theoretical background

1.1 The rise of adaptation studies

In his celebrated work "The Death of the Author" Roland Barthes suggests that "a text is not a line of words releasing a single "theological meaning" (the "message" of the Author-God) but a multi-dimensional space in which a variety of writings, none of them original, blend and clash." In the same work, Barthes defines the text as "a tissue of quotations drawn from the innumerable centers of culture." (146) Barthes's words reflect a dynamic understanding of textuality defining the text in its interaction between many cultural contexts. Similarly Jacques Derrida argues "there is nothing outside of the text" (158), which indicates that all texts refer to themselves and one another. As Barthes and Derrida's suggestions neglect the idea of an original text, they situate the text on an ongoing process of "writ[ing]" (Barthes 4) or "differance," in between "difference" and "deferral" (Derrida 28). This poststructuralist perspective towards text has been very influential in understanding the ontology of text as well as in recognizing multiple levels of interaction between different texts or within different layers of the same text. Barthes's arguments in his work entitled "Death of the Author: The Birth of the Reader" has greatly contributed in refiguring the writer of a certain text as also a reader of a previously written text and thus in depolarizing the distinction between the writer and the reader. Given this perspective, any text is inevitably self-referential and in Barthes's poststructuralist sense or Julia Kristeva's semiotic understanding, it is also "intertextual" (69), which in turn manifests its potential rewritability.

Another noteworthy contribution has been made by Linda Hutcheon who considers "postmodern parody" as "ironic quotation, pastiche, appropriation and intertextuality," which intends to visit the past representations from a "critical" stance rather than a "nostalgic" yearn. (93) Hutcheon's views on postmodern parody are very relevant to the context of rewrite in which the rewriter gets involved in an intertextual relation with an already written text, thus intending to build a bridge between the past and the present. Here it may be crucial to note that rewrite differs from intertextuality because it requires an intentional dialogue with another text. Drawing on

Hutcheon's words, it may be argued that any type of rewrite is an effective tool for what she calls "subver[sion]" as well as "legitimi[zation]," involving both "deconstruc[tion]" and "[re]construc[tion]" as it intends to be to "critical" as well as "creative." (101) Given this context, the key word subversion involves a strong discourse, implying thematic and technical challenge together. Andre Lefevere reads rewriting as a "manipulat[ive]" strategy to offer the source text in a discourse which goes parallel to the current ideologies of the target culture. (8) Rewriting has recently become one of the most demanded modes of writing. Edward Said emphasizes the growing tendency for rewriting as "the writer thinks less of writing originally, and more of rewriting." (157) Lefevere and Said's words both underline the significance of rewrite in shaping and projecting contemporary cultures.

The origins of adaptation can be traced to classical parody, which dates back to classical antiquity. Aristotle's *Poetics* includes references to parody as a genre imitating epic. Mock epic can be considered the most popular genre in Italian literature during the 17th century and in British literature during the Augustan Age. Linda Hutcheon suggests that "[l]ike parodies, adaptations have an overt and defining relationship to prior texts, usually revealingly called "sources." Unlike parodies, however, adaptations usually openly announce this relationship." (3) Although it should be noted that classical parody and adaptation are two different genres, both are written by rewriters, revisiting an already-existing text by a canonical writer with a critical stance.

The term adaptation was introduced with the flourishing of film adaptations of literary works towards the end of the 19th century. Although the term is now being used in a broader sense, adaptation is initially associated with screening. Imelda Whelehan puts forth that for the last two decades, there has been an increasing interest in text to screen adaptations and "fidelity" to the adapted text has usually been a critical point of evaluation. (3) In this respect, film adaptation is being placed into a second category as opposed to the privileged positioning of the source text. In Whelehan's words, "for many people," there is inevitably an "unconscious prioritizing" of the "originary text" over "its film version." (3)

Another significant debate in adaptation studies has been on the inter-semiotic transfer process in stage to screen adaptations. Since theater is a performative genre which draws on "showing," some scholars argue that it is easier to make a film out of a play rather than a novel, while others claim that in most of the cases, the film remains only as a screened play due to the gap between different sign systems and technologies. In fact it may be claimed that the juxtaposition of two different understandings of showing would be a considerable challenge. Deborah Cartmell suggests that "adaptations of texts to screen" are "historically privileged" as she supports her argument with references to the Academy Awards. (23, 24) Cartmell's words also imply that text to screen transfer usually functions better, which in turn can be linked to reading and watching being thoroughly different experiences and thus, not rivals.

As 1960s translation studies shifted from a source-oriented approach to a target-oriented understanding, also owing to Homi K. Bhabha's conception of "cultural translations" (226–227), a new interdisciplinary field, "adaptation studies" flourished in the 1970s. The translation studies scholar Andre Lefevere considers translation as an act of "rewrite" (vii), a broad term which includes adaptations as well. While Lefevere he defines "rewrite" as "manipulation, undertaken in the service of power [...]" (vii), he adds that no matter the target, any act of rewriting inevitably manifests its own "ideology" and "manipulate[s] literature to function in a given society in a given way." (vii) Given this context, an adaptation is noted as a different type of rewrite than translation, although they share some common characteristics such as their ideological and manipulative functions.

With the rise of above-mentioned poststructuralist theories, the writer's privileged position on the text is gradually challenged and eventually replaced by reader-centered criticisms. These theoretical developments justify the grounds for "free" adaptations as well, locating the reader and the subjective reading process at the center of the text. Since the adapter is both the reader and the critic of the source text, his/her reception of the text becomes doubly privileged. The adapter is however different than the translator, as his/her major concern is specifically "adapting" the source text.

Another influential perspective on the flourishing of adaptations is inevitably the performance theories of Erica Fischer-Lichte and Susan Bassnet-McGuire, which, owing to its performativity, treat the dramatic text within the contexts of dramaturgy and theater translation as always dynamic and ongoing. (Fischer-Lichte 9, Bassnet-McGuire 1980:107–128) Their theories therefore view the "signifying" process as an intergeneric encounter between the written text and its possible performances in variable contexts. In Özden Sözalan's words, "[d]ramatic writing is a distinctive form of literary production because it is already impregnated with its own potential materialisation, and so it unsettles the opposition between word and action, mind and body." (11) At the crossroads between literature and performance, writing and showing, reading and watching; the dramatic text can be considered "hybrid" in form and with its everlasting potential to be staged in unlimited times, spaces and other possible contexts, also "adaptive."

Adaptation is by its dictionary definition, "to make suitable" to another context which inevitably requires an intercultural or intergeneric transfer. To Linda Hutcheon, adaptation implies "an acknowledged transposition of a recognizable work in a process of creation and reception" (8), involving both "difference" and "repetition." (114) An earlier theorist, Geoffrey Wagner, classifies adaptation as "transposition, commentary and analogue." (20–21) In this respect, adaptation is a translational and analytical process which requires an intentional engagement with the source text, offering new interpretive contributions. In a broader sense, adaptation is the text meant for the target context and thus the outcome of any intercultural encounter. Focusing on its dialogue with different "medium[s]," Imelda Whelehan views adaptation studies as a "hybrid" kind of study. (3) Similarly Julie Sanders builds on Homi K. Bhabha and considers adaptation as a "hybridized form." (17–19) Its "hybridity" owes to its translational status in between not only two genres or two disciplines but also two different cultural contexts. To put it in Linda Hutcheon's words, "an adaptation has its own aura." (6)

As mentioned above, the question of "fidelity versus betrayal" to the source text has been the major point of departure for many adaptation studies scholars. Some suggest that the adapter should be careful while in such a dialogue with a canonical work, whereas others argue on the side of "free adaptations." As Linda Hutcheon puts it, "[a]daptation is repetition, but repetition without replication." (7) as well as "[...] a derivation that is not derivative -a work that is second without being secondary." (9) Drawing on Hutcheon's words which do not undermine the "creative" and "interpretive" process in such "acknowledged transpositions" (8), the functions of free or loose adaptations or "appropriations" can be justified.

26

Appropriations are free adaptations involving more secondary relation with more indirect reference to the source text as compared to other types of adaptations. As Julie Sanders explains their difference in her theoretical work entitled *Adaptation and Appropriation*, she suggests: "[A]ppropriation frequently affects a more decisive journey away from the informing source into a wholly new cultural product and domain." (Sanders 27) Sanders's use of the term "appropriation" is as if a different term outside adaptations has been criticized by certain adaptation studies scholars. In her seminal work entitled *Novel Shakespeares: Twentieth-Century Women Novelists and Appropriation*, Sanders discusses different understandings of the term "appropriation" with references to Daniel Fischlin and Mark Fortier's preference to use the word "adaptation" which sounds "less negative" as compared to "appropriation" in their edition of plays based on Shakespearean drama. (1, 2) Sanders quotes Fischlin and Fortier's argument that the term "appropriation" implies "a hostile take-over, a seizure of authority over the original" and juxtaposes their perspective with those of Christy Desmet and Robert Sawyer who read the same term as a sign of creativity and criticism. (Sanders 1, 2) In *Novel Shakespeares*, Sanders asserts that her use of the term broadly involves both "the process of textual take over and adaptation." (3) The translation studies scholars also point out the significance of the rewriter's ideology and perspective in classifying certain works as translations or indigenous works. For instance, Şehnaz Tahir Gürçağlar refers to "the appropriation of foreign characters, the indifference towards the authorial provenance of the [original] works and the lack of a clear-cut distinction between translated and indigenous works" (259) as parameters in distinguishing the rewriterly process.

The popularization of adaptation studies goes in accordance with the contemporary movements. Especially the rise of postcolonial and feminist theories, which historically went parallel to the poststructuralist movements, have foregrounded the need for an alternative genre which would revisit the past with a new perspective. The counter-oppressive arguments provided by these discourses inevitably challenge the existing structures including the forms and genres of writing as well as the canon itself. While patriarchal and colonial contexts of many classical works are increasingly challenged in contemporary times, adaptation has proven itself as a very effective genre in communicating the desire to "dehistoricise" the past.

By the same token, adaptation studies has become the rising discipline of the last few decades, drawing on both comparative literature as well as interdisciplinary studies and inevitably reinforced by oppression resistant discourses of contemporary times.

1.2 Adapting Shakespeare: "A Tribute or A Challenge To Canonical Authority"?

Adaptation, appropriation and Shakespeare have always been interrelated throughout literary history because Shakespeare is a successful appropriator himself and his legacy foregrounds him as the most appropriated playwright. It is now a common knowledge that Shakespeare has used history and mythology as noteworthy reference points in his drama. *Ur-Hamlet* and *King Leir*, for instance, were recycled from then contemporary anonymous plays while a considerable part of *Othello* was based on the 16th century Italian writer Cinthio's short story *Un Capitano Moro; The Foolish Captain* in English translation. Shakespeare's authorial revision has been a much debated issue from 1725 onwards, from when, in his *Preface to Shakespeare*, Alexander Pope originally suggested that Shakespeare was a "double" reviser of both his own works and those of other writers, to our contemporary times. In her comprehensive study titled *Revising Shakespeare*, Grace Iopollo makes a distinction between 'theatrical adaptation' and 'authorial revision', relating the latter to Shakespeare's act in reworking his and his predecessors' works (20), usually after performance. (154)

Shakespeare has also been noted as the most recycled playwright of all ages, from his contemporaries to our contemporaries. The earliest recorded rewrite of Shakespeare's plays is John Fletcher's sequel to *The Taming of the Shrew* as *The Woman's Prize; or the Tamer Tamed* in 1611. Fletcher's adaptation was based on John Dryden and William Davenant's remake of *The Tempest* as *The Tempest or the Enchanted Island* in 1670 and William Davenant's adaptations of *Measure for Measure* (1673) as *The Law Against Women* and *Macbeth* as *Macbeth*. (1674) David Garrick's *Hamlet* (1772), Johann Wolfgang Goethe's *Romeo and Juliet* (1812), John Keats's unfinished work *King Stephen: A Dramatic Fragment* (1819) and Maurice Dowling's *Othello Travestie* (1839) are among the noteworthy pioneers of rewriting Shakespearean plays.

Twentieth-century drama witnessed many adaptations, some of which are appropriations of Shakespeare. The long list includes Percy MacKayne's *Caliban by the Yellow Sands* (a 1916 adaptation of *The Tempest*), Gordon Bottomley's *Gruach* (adapting *Macbeth*, in 1922), Federico Garcia Lorca's *The Public* (adapting *Romeo and Juliet*, 1929–1930), Bertolt Brecht's *Roundheads and Peakheads* (adapting *Measure for Measure*, in 1936), Tom Stoppard's *Rosencrantz and Guildenstern Are Dead* as an existentialist adaptation of Hamlet, in 1967), Aime Cesaire's *A Tempest* (a 1969 adaptation of *The Tempest* in postcolonial context), Murray Carlin's *Not Now, Sweet Desdemona* (a South African adaptation of *Othello*, in 1969), Welcome Msomi's *uMabatha* (a Zulu adaptation of *Macbeth*, in 1970), Eugene Ionesco's *Macbett* (a 1972 adaptation, a comedy), Heiner Müller's *Macbeth* (1972), Charles Marowitz's *Measure for Measure* (1975), Tom Stoppard's *The Fifteen-Minute Hamlet* (a 1976 adaptation), Heiner Müller's *Hamletmachine* (1977), Ken Mitchell's *Cruel Tears* (adapting *Othello*, in 1977), Charles Marowitz's *A Macbeth* (in 1978), Tom Stoppard's *Dogg's Hamlet, Cahoot's Macbeth* (in 1979), Carmelo Bene's *Richard III* (an avant-garde adaptation in 1979) which was accompanied by Gilles Deleuze's theories in *Superpositions* (1979), Melissa Murray's *Ophelia* (1979), Alison Lyssa's *Pinball* (1981, appropriating *King Lear*), Herbert Blau's *Elsinore: An Analytical Scenario*, *The Sea* by Edward Bond (adapting *The Tempest*, in 1982), Derek Walcott's *A Branch of the Blue Nile* (a postcolonial adaptation of *Antony and Cleopatra*, 1986), The Women's Theatre Group and Elaine Feinstein's collaborated production entitled *Lear's Daughters* (1987), Philip Osment's *This Island's Mine* (1987), Nicholas Abraham's *The Phantom of Hamlet* (1988), David Malouf's *Blood Relations* (1988), Howard Barker's *7 Lears* (1990), *Lion in the Streets* by Judith Thomson (adapting *Hamlet*, 1990), *Goodnight Desdemona (Good Morning Juliet)* by Ann-Marie MacDonald (a feminist adaptation of *Othello* and *Romeo and Juliet*, 1990), Charles Marowitz's adaptation of *Julius Caesar* as published in *Recycling Shakespeare* (1991), Norman Chaurette's *The Queens* (adapting *King Richard the Third*, 1992), Paula Vogel's *Desdemona: A Play About A Handkerchief* (1993), Ken Gass's *Claudius* (adapting *Hamlet*, 1995), Djanet Sears's *Harlem Duet* (adapting *Othello*, 1997) and Toni Morrison's *Desdemona* (adapting *Othello*, 2012).

A careful examination of the above list indicates that women playwrights have started adapting Shakespeare only after the 1980s, and the number of adaptations by contemporary women playwrights have started to increase very recently. This subject is left for a further discussion in I.4. Another noteworthy point is the growing interest in adapting Shakespeare especially after the 1960s, which overlaps with the rise of poststructuralist and postcolonial theories.

The British attitude towards Shakespeare can be viewed as more conservative than international approaches and can be traced to Shakespeare's association with the canonization of their national literature. One can recall the Stratford-upon-Avon origined Royal Shakespeare Productions of many of Shakespeare's history and comedy plays among loyal adaptations. In "Political criticism of Shakespeare," Walter Cohen notes that English critics reinforce "[...] the tradition of using Shakespeare as national icon of conservative continuity" respond to it in a "class conscious" context. (21) Cohen's suggestion accounts for the reason why several noteworthy British adaptations challenge the hierarchical markers in the tradition Shakespearean drama represents. Although comparatively less, British theater has also accommodated such loose adaptations of Shakespeare including the Women's Theatre Group productions; Tom Stoppard and Edward Bond's free adaptations of *Hamlet*, *Macbeth* and *King Lear*, respectively, into philosophical and political contexts.

Revisiting Shakespeare, especially his tragedies, with contemporary consciousness has especially appealed to postcolonial and feminist critics in an intention to challenge the stereotypical representations of the past. Parallel to postmodernist wave, after the 1950s, indigenous film projects, of especially *Hamlet*, have been popularized. To exemplify, one can note the Indian director Kishore Saho's 1954 film production of *Hamlet*, Japanese director Akira Kurosawa's 1960 film *The Bad Sleep Well* and the Turkish director Metin Erksan's 1976 film *Kadın Hamlet/İntikam Meleği* (*Female Hamlet/Angel of Vengance*), all of which loosely follow the Shakespearean plot. Given this context, the 2014 Indian crime drama film production of *Hamlet* titled *Haider*, directed by Vishal Bhardwaj, is also noteworthy to show the continuity of such interest. The South African dramatist Welcome Msomi's Zulu *Macbeth* titled *Umabatha* (1970), the German playwright and theater director Heiner Müller's Hamletmachine (1977) and the Turkish writer Ümit Kıvanç's 1991 publication of *Macbeth. Muhitimize Uyarlama Denemesi (Macbeth. An attempt to adapt into our circle)* can be considered among examples of similar intercultural adaptations.

- Shakespearean tragedies in specific have drawn more intercultural interest. Among the most translated works by Shakespeare, one can easily note his tragedies. While the post 1960s theories in translation studies favor a target culture centered approach, the two terms "cultural translation" and "intercultural adaptation" frequently overlap. To exemplify, having translated Shakespeare's sonnets, *Hamlet* and *A Midsummer Night's Dream* into Turkish, Can Yücel, a well-known contemporary Turkish poet and translator, considers himself as a rewriter rather than a translator. (Karantay 16) His free translation of the famous soliloque "To be, or not to be: that is the question" in *Hamlet* Act III Scene 1 is frequently quoted by both literature and translation studies authorities within the context of "creative writing" in "translation": "Bir ihtimal daha var, o da ölmek mi dersin?" (67) Reminding the Turkish readers and audiences of the lyrics of a classical Turkish song, Yücel makes an adaptive choice to evoke the same effect.

Contemporary "Revising Shakespeare" projects have been supported in the States and Canada as well, since connectedness with or separation from Shakespeare also links to the perception of their cultural identities in relation to the Anglo-European background. As for the Canadian receptions of Shakespeare, which in turn can be taken as signifiers of Canada's ambivalent identity, they define themselves through both continuity and difference from the European origin. In Mark Fortier's words,

> [T]here is always something un-Canadian, about being Canadian, that the from elsewhere is part of the being here. Shakespeare, therefore, is one manifestation of the from elsewhere at work in Canada. As such, Canadians confront Shakespeare as the cultural undead, neither dead nor living, not a person but an other forming part of living personalities [...] the otherness of the past the remains of which reside here. (342)

It is very noteworthy that adaptation studies had its early rise in Canada which is the two contemporary adaptation theorists Linda Hutcheon and Deborah Cartmell's country of origin. Parallel to that Canada accommodates many adaptors of Shakespeare including Margaret Atwood, Ken Mitchell,

Edward Folger, Djanet Sears and Ann-Marie MacDonald. Michael D. Bristol acknowledges that "Shakespeare has been recognized as an institution in America" (203) while the name signifies "resistence to coercive authority" (204) at the same time. Walter Cohen argues, while Marxist criticism is more influential in post-1980 Shakespeare studies in UK, the American scholars of Shakespeare reflect their "national and geographical distance from Shakespeare" (21) onto their new historicist and feminist perspectives on Shakespeare. (19) Both on stage and screen, the States introduced a remarkable number of adaptors of Shakespeare, among which one can recall Charles Marowitz, Jane Smiley, Paula Vogel and Toni Morrison *Desdemona*s as well as several film directors. While the American continent has obviously had a special interest in Shakespeare's representation of the black identity, Caliban in *The Tempest* and Othello in *The Tragedy of Othello, The Moor of Venice* have been located at the center of postcolonial attention.

Adaptors of Shakespeare usually favor tragedy, the subject matter of which, human misery, appeals to a wider range of readers and audiences. Another reason may be that transferring the catharsis, without spoiling the effect to contemporary or intercultural readers or audiences, sets forth a more objective criteria for the adaptation process. As for Shakespeare's history plays, abroad, they may not be received with the same interest. On the other hand, adapting Shakespearean comedies implies a more difficult transfer since humor is usually received as time or culture specific. Outside the genre of tragedy, *The Tempest* is exceptionally adaptive probably because of its colonial implications or owing to its intergeneric qualities as a tragicomedy. As Julie Sanders notes, together with *Hamlet* and *The Tempest*, *Othello* can be considered among the most frequently adapted plays by Shakespeare. (64–68) Besides, a considerable number of well-known contemporary women writers including Gloria Naylor, Iris Murdoch, Kate Atkinson, Jane Smiley, Marina Warner and Angela Carter have adapted Othello into novel. Naylor's African-American context in *Mama Day*, a comprehensive study of these novels is offered in Julie Sanders's book *Novel Shakespeares: Twentieth-Century Women Novelists and Appropriation* (2001).

It may be crucial to note that there is also a remarkable number of novel and film adaptations of Shakespeare's plays as much as those in poetry, which are not included in this study, selectively focusing on theater. However, some of the very valuable scholarly work on these subjects, such as Deborah Cartmell's *Interpreting Shakespeare on Screen* (2000) and Julie Sanders's book *Novel Shakespeares: Twentieth-Century Women Novelists and Appropriation* (2001) have been visited since they involve several relevant discussions on revisiting Shakespeare in feminist and postcolonial contexts.

Shakespeare has inevitably become the most foregrounding figure for the recently popularized literary trend in rewriting the classics. An increasing number of contemporary researchers published books or chapters on adapting Shakespeare which have greatly contributed to both Adaptation and Shakespeare Studies. Jean Marsden's work entitled *The Appropriation of Shakespeare* (1991), *Transforming Shakespeare: Contemporary Women's Re-Visions in Literature and Performance* edited by Marianne Novy (1999), *Shakespeare and Appropriation* edited by Christy Desmet and Robert Sawyer (1999), Thomas Cartelli's *Repositioning Shakespeare: National formations, postcolonial appropriations* (1999), *Adaptations of Shakespeare: A Critical Anthology of plays from the seventeenth century to the present* edited by Daniel Fischlin and Mark Fortier (2000), Julie Sanders's "'Here's a strange alteration': Shakespearean Appropriations" published in *Adaptation and Appropriation* (2006), *Borrowers and Lenders: The Journal of Shakespeare and Appropriation* (2007), Margaret Jane Kidnie's *Shakespeare and The Problem of Adaptation* (2009), which offer innovative perspectives on contemporary text-to-text or text-to-stage adaptations of Shakespearean drama are specifically noteworthy besides numerous valuable sources on novel and screen adaptations of Shakespeare.

In her groundbreaking work *A Theory of Adaptation*, Linda Hutcheon puts forth that adaptations of classics are usually "intended as tributes or as a way to supplant canonical cultural authority." (93) Most of the contemporary playwrights revisiting Shakespeare follow similar adaptive methods. They either own a loyal perspective foregrounding the significance of the Shakespearean source text or a challenging attitude towards Shakespeare, announcing that the adaptation is nearly an innovation, only inspired by the source text. In other words, adapting Shakespeare in contemporary times usually implies either a yearning for the past or a search for alternating the past. However, in both cases, thematic intertextuality is often accompanied by an experimental form which the genre of adaptation inevitably accommodates. Borrowing Julie Sanders's words, adaptation is a "hybridized form" (18), or a separate genre which is the outcome of a metatextual encounter between past and present, and between "continuity" and "difference" (Hutcheon 2001:93). Therefore, adaptation owns a complicated ontological status, especially given the context of Shakespeare who metaphorically stands for the standards of dramatic form as well as a break away from the dramatic form of classical antiquity. In other words, reading Shakespeare requires an in-depth involvement in different modes of adaptation not only because we are still adapting Shakespeare in contemporary times but also because Shakespeare himself adapted the classical period. In this respect, it is necessary to remind the question Linda Hutcheon poses; do classical adaptations aim at "tribute[s]" or rather to "supplant the canonical figure of cultural authority"? (93)

1.3 Women writers adapting Shakespearean tragedies

In her seminal essay published in 1929, one of the earliest feminist theorists and writers, Virginia Woolf argues that if Shakespeare had a sister with the same talent and wit, she would not have had the opportunities to become a writer. (47–49) Woolf's work inspired many later feminist theorists such as Elaine Showalter, who in her celebrated book *A Literature of Their Own* (1977) traces British fiction writers from the Bronte sisters to Dorris Lessing. Manifesting her response to Virginia Woolf's *A Room of One's Own* in its choice of the title, Showalter's work announces the presence of Shakespeare's sisters in literary canon. Introduced in the 1970s, the French feminist critics' notion of "Eccriture feminine" (women's writing), which ultimately suggests that a new language and even a new form of writing is required to account for the experience of the female body (Cixous 253), has inspired many contemporary women writers to use experimental forms. Perhaps because to challenge the form and structures inevitably implies challenging the existing canon, a remarkable number of women writers tried their hands in revisiting Shakespeare in a new form.

In her in-depth work entitled *Novel Shakespeares: Twentieth-Century Women Novelists and Appropriation*, Julie Sanders poses the question "what politics are at stake when women revise Shakespeare in the form of a prose narrative" (3) and seeks an answer by examining a long list of groundbreaking novels including Barbara Trapido's *Juggling* (appropriating

A Midsummer Night's Dream), Angela Carter's *Wise Children* (appropriating multiple comedies and tragedies by Shakespeare), Kate Atkinson's *Human Croquet* (appropriating comedies by Shakespeare), Erica Jong's *Serenissima* (appropriating *The Merchant of Venice*), Iris Murdoch's *The Black Prince* (appropriating *Hamlet*) and *Sea, Sea* (appropriating *The Tempest*), Marina Warner's *Indigo: or, Mapping the Waters,* Leslie Forbes's *Bombay Ice* (revisiting *The Tempest*), Gloria Naylor's *Mama Day* (revisiting *The Tempest*), Jane Smiley's *A Thousand Acres* (appropriating *King Lear*), Valerie Miner's *A Walking Fire* (appropriating *King Lear*), Lucy Ellman's *Sweet Desserts* (appropriating *King Lear*) and Margaret Atwood's *Cat's Eye* (appropriating *King Lear*). Sanders's comprehensive study puts forth women writers' growing interest in appropriating Shakespearean plays and their challenging attitudes in "revis[ing]" them in a new understanding as well as another form.

There is a noteworthy rise in the number of adaptations of Shakespearean plays by women playwrights in contemporary times as well. It may be also meaningful to note that most of the Shakespearean plays adapted by women playwrights are tragedies. Tragedy is the oldest genre to define its parameters by the time Aristotle's *Poetics* was written, around 335 BC. This is perhaps one of the reasons why women playwrights appropriating Shakespeare prefer to rewrite his tragedies rather than his comedies or history plays, in order to go back and revisit the oldest accessible form of representation in contemporary understanding. As discussed earlier, adaptation is a "hybrid" genre owing to its intertextual and interdisciplinary characteristics.

Relating to the before-mentioned feminist call for a new form to express female experience, adaptation can easily serve as that new form because it ontologically requires a dialogue with previous forms, both as their inheritor and as their rival. Perhaps adaptation has thus become a very convenient form of writing especially for women writers who want to revisit the past and rewrite themselves into it. Appropriating tragedies by Shakespeare therefore sets a fascinating ground for women playwrights who wish to restage Shakespearean plays, re-representing their female protagonists. This study uses the term "appropriation" synonymously with loose adaptation and revision, drawing on Julie Sanders's previously mentioned understanding of the word as a critical journey away from the source text and Adrienne Rich's decolonizing perspective embedded in her terminology.

According to the feminist understanding of Rich, which may also be applicable to postcolonial perspective, revising a canonical text with a new interpretation is necessary not to visit the past nostalgically but rather to challenge its oppressive markers on our contemporary visions:

> Re-vision-the act of looking back, of seeing with fresh eyes, of entering an old text from a new critical direction-is for us more than a chapter in cultural history; it is an act of survival. Until we can understand the assumptions in which we are drenched we cannot know ourselves... We need to know the writing of the past, and know it differently than we have ever known it; not to pass on a tradition but to break its hold over us. (35)

In her feminist work *Transforming Shakespeare: Contemporary Women's Re-Visions in Literature and Performance*, Marianne Novy also uses the term "re-vision" in the sense of "demythologiz[ing]" the stories of patriarchal cultures. (1, 2) Given this context, loose or free adaptations, transformations, revisions and appropriations can be viewed as adaptations or rewrites of an earlier text introducing a certain context, perspective or ideology, respectively. It needs to be highlighted that while loose or free adaptations considerably add to and omit from the source text by underlining a specific context, it has a softer address as compared to the latter three.

One of the pioneers of this trend is *Lear's Daughters* (1987), a prequel to Shakespeare's *King Lear*, in which The Women's Theatre Group, a contemporary British theater company renowned for feminist productions collaborated with Elaine Feinstein, a contemporary British writer and translator. The feminist play appropriates *King Lear* by not representing and in turn challenging the presence of King Lear throughout the play. The play, on the other hand, successfully develops the characterization of the three daughters and manifests its feminist intentions by rewriting the title as *Lear's Daughters*. The play which Lizbeth Goodman calls "a landmark in feminist 'reinventing' of Shakespeare" (220), has provided an inspirational ground for the later women playwrights.

The Canadian playwright Judith Thompson has made another significant contribution to the female canon appropriating Shakespeare as she premiered her two-act play *Lion in the Streets* (1990). Thompson's play, which is an outcome of the first public workshop project initiated in 1990 in Toronto, revisits *Hamlet* as its female protagonist, the ghost of a nine-year-old Portuguese girl called Isobel, tries to find out her murderer among her own circle. *Lion in the Streets* is a striking work which definitely calls for feminist readers.

The above-mentioned women playwrights have chosen to appropriate well-known tragedies by Shakespeare, named after their male protagonists. Both *King Lear* and *Hamlet* are criticized by feminist critics for employing certain patriarchal themes. For instance, Hamlet's first soliloquy in Act 1 Scene 2, "Frailty thy name is woman," is frequently being criticized for "misogyny;" Kathleen McLuskie argues the presence of a "misogynistic" content in the negative representations of Goneril and Regan in *King Lear*. Ophelia and Gertrude's instrumental presences in *Hamlet* resemble those of Goneril and Regan as all these female characters remain secondary to the central plot. Cordelia is distinctly the most developed female character among them; yet, even her "redeeming power" recentralizes the "masculine power" since all her efforts end up in a final father-daughter reconciliation. (McLuskie 99–102) In this respect, both plays have left room for possible feminist readings and in turn rewrites.

Othello has been the most appropriated play by Shakespeare, given the context of contemporary women playwrights. What lies underneath the tragic consequences of the marriage between an aristocratic girl, Desdemona, and the "black" Moor of Venice, Othello, other than simply the villainy of Iago has wondered especially women playwrights.

1.4 Adaptivity of Othello or *Othello*

Andrew Cecil Bradley calls Othello "the greatest poet of all Shakespeare's heroes" (59) while according to Robert Heilman "Othello is the least heroic of Shakespeare's tragic heroes." (166) Despite their different perspectives on *Othello*, critics agree on the everlasting effect of the play on audiences of all times and all cultures. While the beautiful language captures our souls, the realistic representation does so to our minds:

> Othello: Soft you, a word or two before you go:
>   I have done the State some service, and they know 't:
>   No more of that. I pray you in your letters,
>   When you shall these unlucky deeds relate,
>   Speak of me, as I am. Nothing extenuate,
>   Nor set down aught in malice.
>   Then you must speak,

Of one that lov'd not wisely, but too well:
Of one, not easily jealous, but being wrought,
Perplex'd in the extreme: Of one, whose hand
(Like the base Indian) threw a pearl away
Richer than all his tribe: Of one whose subdu'd eyes,
Albeit unused to the melting mood,
Drops tears as fast as the Arabian trees
Their medicinable gum. Set you down this:
And say besides, that in Aleppo once,
Where a malignant, and a turban'd Turk
Beat a Venetian, and traduc'd the State,
I took by th' throat the circumcised dog,
And smote him, thus. (Act V, Scene II)

The above quote, in a very effective poetic language, displays Othello's call for a realistic storytelling. He wishes to be remembered not for his heroic actions but rather as a man with his faults and failures.

The same quote also represents Othello's internalized blackness. As Othello calls Desdemona "a pearl richer than all his tribe," this perspective comes out. Similarly, he uses "the Arabian trees" simile, which can be read as a signifier of his race, as he refers to his tears falling down.

Othello talks about racism without centralizing the issue of race as its major subject. The contemporary critic Virginia Mason Vaughan emphasizes Othello as a "profoundly political drama" (6) while the black scholar S.E. Ogude notes that "[...] every production of Othello is a reenactment of racial tensions, and Othello is preeminently a caricature of the black man." (163) Although a noteworthy number of critics read *Othello* as a "racist" play drawing on the racist representations of Iago and Roderigo, which finally victimize the dark-skinned Othello, several scholars like Karen Newman argue that *Othello* reflects Shakespeare's resistance to oppressive markers, including race:

> Shakespeare was certainly subject to the racist, sexist and colonialist discourses of its time, but by making the black Othello a hero, and by making Desdemona's love for Othello, and her transgression of her society' norms for women in choosing him, sympathetic, Shakespeare's play stands in contestatory relation to the hegemonic ideologies of race and gender in early modern England (Newman 219),

As Newman's above lines indicate, Shakespeare in *Othello*, offers an insight on the existing gender and racial oppression in his time England. His representation of Othello as a successful soldier and a passionate lover, exceptionally, challenges the stereotypical representations of the black race. Criticizing the modern critics, including the well-known Shakespeare scholar A.C. Bradley, for their "anti-Othello" stance, Abdulla Al-Dabbagh argues that Shakespeare "reverses" the racial stereotypes through *Othello*. (16, 17) Similar to Newman's genderly focus, Al-Dabbagh reads "Shakespeare's sympathetic identification" with the protagonist and his representation of racism as Iago, Othello's antagonist, as the playwright's reaction to the racist context of those times' England. (17) In this respect, one may relate Shakespeare's target for identification with the protagonist to his search for an innovative type of "catharsis," which operates by creating an awareness on racism in the audience. Different from the Aristotelian understanding of "catharsis," which works by evoking a collective "purification" and "purgation," Shakespeare's strategy perhaps aims at individual questionings.

Despite their different emphases, many critics agree that *The Tragedy of Othello: The Moor of Venice* is one of the greatest plays in the canon as well as a play with an issue for all times. Having been recycled by Shakespeare from the 16th-century Italian writer Cinthio's short story *Un Capitano Moro* in around 1603, the story of Othello, the black moor, incorporates many universal and everlasting themes such as race, passion, jealousy and revenge. However, it is more the poetic language and the intelligent structure of the play which asserts its irreplaceable presence in the literary canon. *Othello* is also noteworthy among Shakespeare's tragedies as it is presented in both the 1622 Quarto and 1623 Folio, with considerable variations within a remarkably short time. Several critics including David Bevington read *Othello* as a real example of "Shakespearean revision." (510)

The play was revisited many times on stage with different methods such as employing Othello as a female character or offering the play in the form of opera or ballet. Not only performances of *Othello* itself, but also its remakes have received many positive criticism by its contemporary critics. To exemplify, one can recall Maurice Dowling's entertaining play *Othello Travestie* (1839) which is a travesty in ten scenes, based on the Shakespearean play. Dowling's play is considered significant by the critics since it might have inspired many contemporary American and Canadian playwrights including Charles Marowitz (1974), Ken Mitchell (1977), Ann-Marie MacDonald (1990), Paula Vogel (1993), Djanet Sears (1997) and Toni Morrison (2012) to revisit *Othello* in new contexts.

The above-mentioned contemporary playwrights commonly get involved in a free/loose adaptation or appropriation process of the Shakespearean source text. Another noteworthy point is that these playwrights come from either American or Canadian backgrounds. The first American stage production of *Othello* with a black actor in 1943, directed by Margaret Webster, is also worth mentioning as a pioneer of representation of the protagonist as a black character, providing a background for later postcolonial readings of the play in the Americas.

Born in 1934 in the States, Charles Marowitz adapted many plays by Shakespeare, including *Hamlet, MacBeth, the Taming of the Shrew, Measure for Measure* and *the Merchant of Venice*. In 1974, he published *A Othello*, an appropriation of *Othello* in eleven scenes. *An Othello*, with the power of satire, enables to offer a social critique on different types of racism while being loyal to Shakespeare's *Othello* only in using the characters' names. *An Othello* represents Iago as a black character engaging in racial activism while it also centralizes Othello as distinctly black as opposed to the "Snow White Cinderella Marilyn Monroe" Desdemona. (260) The Duke is represented as a Jewish character, manipulated by strong racism, while Desdemona and Cassio are introduced as adulterous figures. *An Othello* also appropriates the play into an American context of racism or the transformation of the national understanding from "melting pot" to "salad bowl." In his study, Abdelrhaffar B. Larbi resembles the Duke and Lodovico's racisms to the white American racist group Ku Klux Klan (151), also pointing out that the play continuously offers references to the American cultural context. (151–158)

Born in 1939, Ken Mitchell is a Canadian writer exploring the Canadian culture in most of his writing. His most celebrated work on stage, *Cruel Tears* (1977), is an appropriation of *Othello* into "prairie context." A French word for meadow, "prairie" is a term used to refer to common characteristics of North American land, usually associated with a harsh landscape. Mitchell's play takes place in a prairie landscape and offers a white Othello with a Ukrainian background, Johnny. The characters in *Cruel Tears* are all white working class people of rural life. Mitchell changes the names of the characters while preserving the main plot as well as some epic qualities of Shakespeare's *Othello*. Giving his characters a distinctly Canadian voice, Mitchell brings into the play a Canadian background of contemporary times.

It may be useful to mention two contemporary American screen adaptations of *Othello*, also offering new Othellos rather than *Othellos*. The 1995 film adaptation *Othello* is noteworthy as the first mainstream cinema production with a black actor, Laurence Fishburn, playing Othello and the celebrated actor and director Kenneth Branagh playing Iago. Although the 1995 production, directed by Oliver Parker, can be considered as a relatively loyal adaptation of Shakespeare's *Othello*, the film adaptation is usually found more "Iago-centric" than the source text. Another striking film adaptation from the States is the 2001 production, O, which is a loose adaptation of *Othello* into contemporary context. Directed by Tim Blake Nelson, O tells a basketball star, Othello (O.J.)'s story as the only African-American student in an American high school. The critical reception of O was usually positive and the actor, Mekhi Phifer, was praised for his performance of Othello. The two contemporary American film adaptations contributed to offer a more realistic representation of Othello in cinema and reach a wider audience.

It is no wonder that the above-mentioned contemporary adapters who chose to adapt *Othello* somehow dealt with the issue of race, especially when postcolonial readings of the text have been on the agenda of many noteworthy critics, drawing on different assumptions of racism in the text (Newman 1987, Bartles 1990, Andreas 1992, Loomba 1992, MacDonald 1994 and Parker 1994). Race is obviously a significant theme in Shakespeare's *Othello* the protagonist of which, in an account of his adventures, tells that he had been once sold as a "slave" and later bought his freedom. (Act I Scene 3) In his conversation with Iago in Act I Scene I, Roderigo reveals his racist perspective, with a note on Othello's physical appearance:

> What a full fortune does the thick-lips owe
> If he can carry't thus!

As he addresses the Moor as simply "the thick-lips," Roderigo's lines above can be read as a strong signifier of black stereotyping. Similarly, Iago's following lines to Brabantio explicitly indicates the presence of a racist perspective directed to the "black" Moor:

> Iago: [...] Even now, now, very now, an old black ram
>   Is tupping your white ewe. Arise, arise;
>   Awake the snorting citizens with the bell,
>   Or else the devil will make a grandsire of you.
>   Arise I say! (Act I Scene 1)

Iago's initial reference to Othello as "old black ram" in contrast to Brabantio's "white ewe" foregrounds the binary opposites of "black" versus "white" and his second reference to Othello as "devil" reminds the reader of accustomed associations of darkness with evil, both implying strong racism. Thomas Cartelli suggests that "Iago is the name Shakespeare gives to the agent of his protagonist's demise, despiser of marriage of races, the wedding of difference" (124) and further notes that similar to Iago, the play "systematically deconstruct[s] the fantasy of interracial and intercultural concord it stages" (125) Given this context, one can read Iago's motivation to ruin Othello's life as racism and relate the unknown reason why he "hate[s] the Moor" (Act I, Scene 3) to strong prejudices and preconditioning towards the Other race. The contemporary critic Virginia Mason Vaughan also views the function of the racial context in Othello very effective in the plot: "The effect of Othello depends, [...], on the essential fact of the hero's darkness, the visual signifier of his Otherness." (51) The "Otherness" of the protagonist Othello, which considerably provokes his white antagonists, can be read as the major reason for his tragic fall. In this respect, Othello can be viewed as a victim of white racism, which in turn reinforces postcolonial interpretations aiming at "decolonizing" his experience.

Feminist critics, on the other hand, are very enthusiastic about reading *Othello* as an anti-feminist text. *Othello* is also foregrounded as a text which embodies a striking amount of gender stereotyping while the two major female characters. A certain feminist criticism focuses on the underdeveloped and stereotypical representations of Desdemona and Emilia, as if "schoolgirls" (Rutter 142), or as "victims of patriarchal marriage conventions." (Vaughan 72) These two women hardly become subjects since they cannot ever act with their individual will, outside the social expectations they were exposed to. The following address of Iago to Brabantio explicitly reflects the ways women are commodified in the text:

> Awake! What, ho, Brabantio! thieves! thieves! thieves!
> Look to your house, your daughter and your bags!
> Thieves! thieves! (Act I Scene 1)

Iago's lines above imply that Brabantio's daughter Desdemona might be stolen, referring to her as if a piece of property. Desdemona's internalization of this patriarchal understanding which views women as objects rather than subjects are also explicit in her following address to her father:

My noble father,
I do perceive here a divided duty:
To you I am bound for life and education;
My life and education both do learn me
How to respect you; you are the lord of duty,
I am hitherto your daughter: but here's my husband,
And so much duty as my mother show'd
To you, preferring you before her father,
So much I challenge that I may profess
Due to the Moor my lord. (Act I Scene 3)

In the above quote, Desdemona asserts that she reconciles with the patriarchal system which transfers her duties towards her father to her husband. Feminist criticism directed to *Othello*, therefore, frequently quotes Desdemona's lines above to show her restrictions under patriarchy as they look for ways to challenge such engendered context.

The above-mentioned racist and misogynistic representations in *Othello* can be traced to the rising contemporary interest in revisiting *Othello* by Shakespeare, from revolutionary perspectives. For instance, the 1995 screen production of *Othello* directed by Oliver Parker, with the black actor Laurence Fishburne as Othello and the well-known Irish actor and director Kenneth Branagh as Iago, is very noteworthy in introducing the first black Othello to mainstream cinema. Although several film authorities considered the film as Iago-centric and thus reductive in its treatment to Othello, Parker's production was very well received by a wide audience. Therefore, *Othello* (1995) made a major contribution in centralizing the racial context of Othello, representing him truly as a black character.

Some stage adaptors such as Iqbal Khan, who has recently directed a challenging Royal Shakespeare Company Production of *Othello*, choose loosely adapting the canonical play into contemporary discourses. The play's major innovation was in representing both Othello and Iago as black and thus blurring the implied racism underlying Iago's villainy. However, the play does not ever undermine the racial context of *Othello*. Khan obviously has an adaptive strategy in making Iago a black racist, resentful to the society he is living in and motivated by both his passion for Desdemona and his desire for power. Khan's production can be viewed as a contemporary liberating appropriation of *Othello* by Shakespeare, although it follows a close dialogue with the source text in the scenes central to the plot. With its anti-oppressive stance manifested in making a disabled actress play the Duke or in improving Emilia's feminist perspective in the last scene, this production effectively challenges the stereotypical representations in *Othello*.

Between 1990 and 2012, Othello was adapted four times by contemporary women playwrights, *Goodnight Desdemona (Good Morning Juliet)* by Ann-Marie MacDonald (1990), Paula Vogel's *Desdemona: A Play About a Handkerchief* (1993), Djanet Sears's *Harlem Duet* (1997) and Toni Morrison's *Desdemona* (2012), following authentic methods and offering different feminist viewpoints. It is noteworthy that these four playwrights commonly dealt with the issue of the handkerchief, foregrounding its significance to the play, despite the distinguishing contents and adaptive strategies of their adaptations.

2 *OTHELLO* and white female body

"I want my students to see Shakespeare's Othello as he is, and to do that, some-
times it might be valuable to see him as someone other than Shakespeare's" (Joyce
Green MacDonald. "Finding Othello's African Roots Through Djanet Sears's
Harlem Duet" 2005:208).

The above quote from Joyce Green MacDonald reflects on the contemporary readers' bias while reading Othello's story across the canonical significance of the play and also justifies the motivations of contemporary
adapters who intend to revisit Othello more than *Othello*. There is a growing interest especially in American and Canadian canons in rethinking the
representation of the protagonist, Othello, in new contexts, parallel to
the theoretical movements after the 1980s. As Joyce Green MacDonald
suggests, the liberty to read Othello as any character without necessarily thinking that he was imagined by the Great Bard, enables the critic
to better recognize Othello's restrictions. This perspective also feeds the
possibility of adapting *Othello* into new cultural contexts, for which there
has been an ever growing interest. This contemporary move to rewrite
Othello inevitably brings into the question Linda Hutcheon poses, do the
adaptive strategies imply "a tribute" or a challenge to "canonical cultural
authority?" (93) This question addresses not only to levels and intentions
of authorial dialogues with the Bard but also (see Chapter 4) to the various
choices of adaptive methods and strategies from a loyal adaptation to an
appropriation or loose adaptation.

Women writers have had a recently rising interest in rewriting *Othello*
in different forms. As mentioned earlier, it is very remarkable that between
1990 and 2012, Othello was revisited by four women playwrights coming
from American or Canadian backgrounds. Feminist criticism has often been
very enthusiastic about reading *Othello* as an anti-feminist text, drawing on
the oppressed representations of female characters. To exemplify, the two
major female characters, Desdemona and Emilia, are frequently considered
among gender stereotypical representations in the play, being more like
"schoolgirls" (Rutter 142) than women and remaining underdeveloped in
characterization. The above mentioned suggestion of misogyny in *Othello*
can be related to contemporary women playwright's growing interest in

revisiting *Othello* by Shakespeare, appropriating the canonical play into contemporary discourses. The underlying context of women's oppression in marital relations parallel to the themes of cuckoldry and jealousy, which is very much present in Shakespeare's *Othello* as it is in most of Elizabethan and Jacobean literature, also strengthens the urge for a feminist rereading.

Among feminist appropriations of *Othello* in contemporary drama written in English language, one can consider *Goodnight Desdemona (Good Morning Juliet)* by Ann-Marie MacDonald (1988), Paula Vogel's *Desdemona: A Play About A Handkerchief* (1993), Djanet Sears's *Harlem Duet* (1997) and Toni Morrison's *Desdemona* (2012). The four contemporary playwrights from the American continent commonly rewrite one of the masterpieces of the European canon with a female emphasis. However, their treatments to women's issue vary parallel to their different understandings of feminism as white lesbian and black or women of color feminism. In turn, their adaptive strategies operate by representing the female subjects and their bodies either within the patriarchal markers of sexuality or within the stereotypical markers of race in a white society. Drawing on the distinguishing lesbian feminist and black feminist perspectives of the four contemporary women writers, Ann-Marie MacDonald, Paula Vogel and Djanet Sears, Toni Morrison, respectively, the different chapters are assigned to discuss the issues of white female sexuality and black female identity. This chapter focuses on the alternative representations of female sexuality in Ann-Marie MacDonald and Paula Vogel's adaptations of *Othello*.

The Canadian writer Ann-Marie MacDonald revisits both *Othello* and *Romeo and Juliet* in her appropriation entitled *Goodnight Desdemona (Good Morning Juliet)*. In the three-act play, MacDonald's contemporary heroine Constance, a dedicated academic, finds out a manuscript which she is convinced to be the original source for Shakespeare's tragedies. In an attempt to explore the manuscript, Constance finds herself among the characters of *Othello* and *Romeo and Juliet*, desperately trying to change the plots to prevent the tragic sequence of events.

At the beginning of the play, Constance reads Othello and Iago's discussion on the handkerchief, which centralizes the handkerchief once again. MacDonald italicizes her quotes from the Shakespearean text, which reflecting an academic style, makes the reader/audience view *Goodnight Desdemona (Good Morning Juliet)* as a literary critique on the Shakespearean text.

With such postmodern consciousness, MacDonald's work offers a striking representation of the contemporary Shakespearean reader as well as the scholar, who besides an intellectual journey to explore the plays, discovers his/her personal quest as reflected onto the reading process.

According to Ric Knowles, Ann-Marie MacDonald's work *Goodnight Desdemona (Good Morning Juliet)* very much reflects the 1980s context of popular culture and "works through a second-wave feminist focus" (145), distinctly emphasizing women's sexual oppression within the family and social life. In the following lines, MacDonald's intellectual heroine Constance announces the reader the underlying feminist concern of MacDonald:

> In both plays [*Rome and Juliet* and *Othello*], the tragic characters, particularly Romeo and Othello, have abundant opportunity to save themselves. The fact that they do not save themselves tends to characterize them as unwitting victims of a disastrous practical joke. Insofar as these plays may be said to be fatalistic at all, any grains of authentic tragedy must be seen to reside in the heroines, Desdemona and Juliet. (8)

In the lines above, MacDonald not only reveals her adaptive strategy in rewriting the two tragedies by Shakespeare, but also accounts for the choice of her title. She also prophesizes that not sleeping Desdemona but awaking Juliet will survive at the end of this process. Actually MacDonald's feminist understanding in *Goodnight Desdemona (Good Morning Juliet)* goes beyond the second-wave feminism and gets closer to the third-wave feminism, for its representation of queer female experience through Juliet and Constance's unexpected emotional and physical attachment in Act III. As Constance asks Juliet if she was from Lesbos (77), she reflects on the accompanying lesbian feminist context of the play.

Although at first sight, entering the fictional world while looking for the lost manuscript, MacDonald's text echoes recurrent patterns of popular cinema and fantasy literature, the play's strong feminist context hardly offers any escape from politics. MacDonald's sarcastic style of writing, which Linda Hutcheon would call "postmodern parody" for its "repetition with critical distance that allows ironic signaling of difference at the very heart of similarity" (185), enables the text to offer a serious content within the mode of comedy. Not "nostalgic" but "creative" revisiting is usually the source of motivation in postmodern parody as Hutcheon puts it forth. Quoted from Constance and Desdemona's conversation in Act II Scene ii, the following lines specifically exemplify the use of postmodern parody in the play:

Desdemona: But tell me more of life in Academe.
If there be cannibals that each other eat,
and men whose heads do grow beneath their shoulders?
These things to hear, I seriously incline.
Constance: It is quite dog eat dog. And scary too.
I've slaved for years to get my doctorate,
but in a field like mine that's so well trod,
you run the risk of contradicting men
who have risen to the rank of sacred cow,
and dying on the horns of those who rule
the pasture with an iron cud. [...] (37)

Desdemona's lines in italics are taken from Desdemona's conversation with Othello in Act I Scene III of the source text. As Desdemona treats academic as a mythical entity, she unconsciously makes an academic reference to an earlier written text which evokes a sense of postmodern comedy. Constance's reply functions similarly by suggesting that there is hardly any difference in power relations inside and outside the text, although at the beginning of the play Constance intended to protect Desdemona against the men in *Othello*. However, Constance, who struggles against the patriarchal context of *Othello*, ends up being oppressed by Desdemona and Juliet's internalized male values:

Desdemona, I thought you were different; I thought you were my friend, I worshipped you. But you're just like Othello-gullible and violent. Juliet, if you really loved me, you wouldn't want me to die. But you were in love with death, 'cause death is easier to love. Never mind. I must have been a monumental fool to think that I could save you from yourselves... Fool... (86–87)

It is ironical that unable to help either herself or Shakespeare's female characters, she notes that in both real life and fiction, women "run the risk of contradicting men who have risen to the rank of sacred cow." In these words, Constance refers to her master and slave relationship with Professor Claude Night, while on another layer she reflects on MacDonald's adaptive authorial dialogue with Shakespeare. As MacDonald's Desdemona repeats Shakespeare's Desdemona's lines in an academic context and MacDonald italicizes Shakespeare's lines which she strategically place in a comic dialogue, the play adheres to Linda Hutcheon's earlier quoted definition of postmodern parody as repeating the past with an interpretive difference. To exemplify, as Desdemona utters Othello's lines for Constance talking to Iago, her lines are italicized; "*If she be false, heaven mocked itself*" (39) while Iago's response which was verbally changed is not placed in italics: "Honest, madam?", "Think?" (39) MacDonald's adaptation, which given this context can also be considered a postmodern parody, of *Othello*, asserts its strength in the revolutionary form it accommodates. From the beginning to the end, MacDonald's play displays being at odds with conventional forms, and thus, makes use of intergeneric and hybrid qualities of 'adaptation'. The intergeneric transfer of a tragedy into a comedy, two genres classical theatre strictly distinguishes, is the major adaptive strategy in the play which is reinforced by the juxtaposition of *Othello* and *Romeo and Juliet* against the principle of unity of subject matter. MacDonald's conscious choice in subverting the play to a point to raise contemporary audience's interest is also considerably fed by her inclusion of reader-response theory as the literary scholar Constance unexpectedly enters the two Shakespearean plays and with active participation effectively changes the flows of events. In this respect, Constance stands for the enthusiastic feminist reader who in the critical reading process struggles with the patriarchal content of the two tragedies and alternatively brings her feminist approach into her reading.

The feminist academic Constance's search for the fool image in the Gustav manuscript, which she thinks turns the tragedies into comedies, alludes to MacDonald's adaptation which turns the two comedies by Shakespeare into a comedy. The well-addressed intergeneric consciousness in MacDonald's adaptation, however, serves as the underlying adaptive strategy rather than an arbitrary postmodern quality:

> I entered, deus ex machina,
> and Desdemona will not die,
> because I dropped in from the sky...
> Does that make this a comedy?
> And does it prove my thesis true?
> In that case, I've preempted the Wise Fool! (33)

In her lines above, Constance realizes that her entrance into the text has an intergeneric function as then the tragedy turns into a comedy. Constance's contemporary intellectual consciousness brings into the text an overall postmodern scope which inevitably accommodates intertextual and intergeneric references and invites reader-response theory. To exemplify the intertextual references in the play, one can note Constance's crossgendering, which is a recurrent element in Shakespearean comedy, besides the play's references to *Hamlet, King Lear* and *Jane Eyre*. (53) There is also a noteworthy reference to the issue of a pre-existing source text and its author in Constance's last remark "In that case I've preempted the Wise Fool!", which in turn reflects on the adaptive strategies and the authorial dialogue. (see Chapter 4) It is also possible to relate the intergeneric shift to the feminist stance of the writer. As Sharon Friedman notes, tragedy, a genre which has usually been identified with the female misery, provides an inescapable ground for feminist resistance (124). Given the context of Shakespeare, one can note that, excluding Lady Macbeth and Cordelia, his tragedies usually offer stereotypical representations of passive female characters, including Desdemona, Gertrude, Ophelia and Juliet. However, Shakespearean comedies introduce more developed female characters such as Kate, Rosalind, Benedick and Portia. This feminist motivation can account for MacDonald's adaptive choice as intergeneric.

The Greek scholar Igor Djordjevic relates the intergeneric qualities of *Goodnight Desdemona (Good Morning Juliet)* to his post-Aristotelian understanding of 'genre transformation' (91), adding Frye's conception of "Augenblick", "crucial moment from which point the road to what might have been and the road to what will be can be simultaneously seen" (Frye 27) into Aristotle's notion of "hamartia". In this respect, one can suggest that MacDonald carefully plays with contemporary audience's possible responses to the tragic flaws of Shakespearean protagonists. As MacDonald simultaneously addresses to contemporary consciousness in a feminist background, any attempt to empathize with the source text protagonists are inevitably represented within the sense of comedy. Constance's search for the fool image in the Gustav manuscript possibly reflects on the contemporary women audiences' quixotic fight to still experience "hamartia", watching a loyal adaptation of Shakespearean tragedies. In other words, *Goodnight Desdemona (Good Morning Juliet)* offers genre transformation for an alternative "hamartia", theirs being postmodern feminist.

The American playwright Paula Vogel employs the handkerchief as a strong signifier of oppression, more specifically hierarchical and gender discrimination in her play *Desdemona: A Play About a Handkerchief*. Vogel rewrites the play centralizing the female characters Desdemona, Emilia and Bianca and dethroning Othello, Iago and Casio in characterization. Vogel's play is often viewed as "a postmodern feminist" reading of Shakespeare's *Othello*. (Peterson and Bennett 341) The play opens with Emilia taking "a white handkerchief" the color reference of which is parallel to its owner Desdemona's aristocracy. Indicating their master and servant relationship, Desdemona asks Emilia to find the handkerchief. The play announces its extreme feminist concerns also by sexualizing the female solidarity, implying a lesbian attachment between Desdemona and Bianca. Vogel's play preserves very little from the Shakespearean play, such as the names of the characters and the final scene in which Emilia brushes Desdemona's hair as Othello gets close to the chamber. Alternatively, the play rereads the handkerchief which in Shakespearean play functions as the instrumental source for tragedy, as a signifier of women's oppression as well as aristocracy and eventually challenges its presence on stage by making Desdemona twist it.

Vogel places the marital institution and gender oppression at the center of a hard discussion by rewriting *Othello* as a thoroughly female play. As Aslı Tekinay puts it forth, "Vogel's play reconfigures the gender politics of 'Othello' by attacking the role of the faithful wife which makes Desdemona a victim." (415) The subversion of Shakespeare's Desdemona as an unfaithful wife not only liberates Desdemona's body but also makes Desdemona truly exist in the existential sense of making a "choice" and bearing its consequences. (Sartre web) In this respect, Vogel's Desdemona acts in accordance with the "subjectivity" and "responsibility" which the existentialist theorist Jean Paul Sartre suggests in his 1946 lectures. In other words, Vogel makes a subject out of Desdemona, who in Shakespearean text is rather Othello's object. For instance, Vogel's Desdemona is represented as an exact non-conformist, enjoying her sexuality freely and courageously: "Stop it, Mealy! Don't be... silly, nothing will happen to me. I'm the sort that will die in bed." (239) Vogel transforms Shakespeare's Desdemona's death in bed which is usually read as a submissive marker signifying gender oppression, into a signifier of female passion. In Sharon Friedman's words, "Vogel's Desdemona is not 'of spirit still and quiet' (I.3.95)." (118) In the above quotation, Friedman draws on Brabantio's description of Desdemona in Act I Scene 3 of *Othello*, where Brabantio also calls Desdemona "A maiden never bold." In this respect, unlike Shakespeare's Desdemona, who by nature is a submissive figure, a prototype for an obedient wife, Vogel's Desdemona is a revolutionary figure, represented unconventionally.

Another issue Vogel's play challenges is the hierarchical oppression among women as represented in Shakespeare's *Othello*. Vogel subverts such hierarchy by equally representing Emilia, Bianca and Desdemona, three white women, a servant, a prostitute and an aristocrat, respectively. By making Bianca and Desdemona work for the same bawdy-house and giving Emilia and Bianca minor ethnic backgrounds, Vogel effectively deconstructs hierarchical stratification between the female characters. To exemplify, in the following lines, Vogel's Emilia reveals lower middle class women's oppression under the marital system, which is reinforced by patriarchy:

> For us in the bottom ranks, when a man and wife hate each other,
>   what is left in a lifetime of marriage but to save and scrimp, plot
>   and plan? I say to him each night- I long for the day you make me
>   a lieutenant's widow. (13)

The same quotation also reflects the hidden desire of Emilia to get rid of Iago and find a new lover, as the reference to John Fowles's novel *The French Lieutenant's Woman* (1969) implies. Emilia also notes that manipulating the male power is the only way of survival for this class of women. Since they cannot control but manipulate their marriage, they cannot be the subjects but rather become objects of their own lives. Given this context, Vogel's adaptive strategy provides Emilia with full motivation to steal and hide the handkerchief, which in the source text starts the tragic sequence of events. The black feminist theorist bell hooks emphasizes the lack of a unified, all inclusive movement called feminism and makes a call for a true female solidarity (5–8), which in turn will considerably contribute to the strength of the movement. Another failing aspect of feminism is put forth by the American feminist Susan Faludi, who suggests that feminism has lost considerable force as women failed to protect their rights as women, falling into the trap of internalized patriarchy. (Faludi ix–xv) Although she differs from Shakespeare's Emilia in being more sincere to Desdemona, Vogel's Emilia still acts as the most conformist female character of the text, until the last three scenes, constantly reminding Desdemona and Bianca of the rules, "You two can cackle with laughter at me if you like, but it's a duty for me to stop your ladyship from gettin' into danger" (248), and refusing to join their conversations on female desire: "I don't understand your 'Adam and Eve' and I don't think I want to...." (248) The lack of female bondage has obviously been the major reason why Shakespeare's

Emilia fails to protect Desdemona against Iago and becomes an instrument for Iago's ill plans. Therefore it is very significant for Vogel's Emilia to pass the test on reliability.

Revisiting Shakespeare's story of the handkerchief, therefore, implies an overall feminist stance which reads the handkerchief also as a signifier of the failure of a sincere female solidarity and resists this situation by rewriting the handkerchief in an alternative, yet still tragic context. While the female characters keep silent, they function within the patriarchal system. Hasine Şen reads female silence as a signifier for their oppression under the "logocentric regime". (2) Given this context, the handkerchief represents women's failure to resist the male order.

Drawing on *Othello*'s plot, Vogel's Emilia steals Desdemona's handkerchief and gives it to Iago, who then passes it to Cassio. Cassio gives the handkerchief to Bianca as a gift, parallel to the sequence of events in the source text. However, although Vogel's Bianca innovatively shows the handkerchief to Desdemona, the tragic consequences cannot be avoided due to women's being insincere to one another. Learning that the handkerchief is Desdemona's, Bianca goes blindly jealous and ironically asks Emilia where Iago was that night Desdemona stood in for her. Emilia does not tell Desdemona where Iago really was. Although Bianca and Desdemona can both tell Iago was setting a bad plan for Desdemona, they keep preparing Desdemona for bed, in turn to death. In other words, Vogel's adaptation keeps Emilia and Bianca responsible for Desdemona's death. Othello, whom Vogel chooses not to represent, only acts as their and Iago's hit man. In this respect, Vogel's adaptive strategy is directed towards foregrounding the story of the handkerchief as a strongly female issue. The handkerchief stands for women's internalization of patriarchy, pointing out the failure of women to protect other women.

The metaphorical enslavement of the white female body also appears as a recurrent theme in Vogel's adaptation and it is further challenged. For instance Desdemona and Emilia realize that Othello was gathering the wedding sheets from their bed, (45) which signifies Desdemona's virginity. In this scene, Desdemona's body and privacy are together captured by Othello, who ironically is obsessed by the white sheet, a signifier of Desdemona's pure and white, female body. However Vogel's Desdemona's body is 'unpure' and 'public', with her free will, which deconstructs the patriarchal associations of female body with private and pure besides the racial context of white-pure association. Vogel's underlying transformative response to the engendered context in the source text is symbolically revealed in her choice of the title. As Vogel consciously addresses, her play represents Desdemona, explicitly, as an actor in the context of the handkerchief and thus transforms the play from being a play about victimization into one on adultery.

On the other hand, the lesbian feminist playwright Paula Vogel treats female sexuality liberally within the borders of the Harem-like ladies' chamber, where Othello cannot be seen but only be heard. Though hesitant at the beginning, Paula Vogel's Desdemona transcends over the boundaries of a patriarchal society and talks freely about sexual experience:

> Desdemona: (Frightened) Emilia, have you ever deceived your husband Iago?
> Emilia (With a derisive snot) That's a good one. Of course not, Miss- I'm an honest woman.
> Desdemona: What does honesty have to do with adultery? Every honest man I know is an adulterer...
> (Pause)
> Have you ever thought about it?
> Emilia: What is there to be thinkin' about it? It's enough trouble once each sunday night, than to be lookin' for it. I'd never cheat –never-not for all the world I wouldn't. (242)

By representing Emilia within the group of women for whom female sexuality is an undesirable and forced experience and implying Desdemona's enjoyment of sexual intercourse, Vogel reminds of the existing class distinction in society, which in turn has led to the failure of feminism to address every woman. Vogel strategically distinguishes between the working class Emilia and the aristocrat Desdemona's experiences of sexuality, as that of objects and subjects respectively, noting that Emilia "despise[s]" (240) her husband while Desdemona yearns for "the first time [she] saw [her] husband and took a glimpse of his skin" (242) As a liberated female character, Vogel's Desdemona shares with Emilia her later regret in marrying Othello; "Ah, Emilia, I should have married Ludovica after all." (241) as well as her former "thrill[ing]" (242) attachment to Othello as a man from another race.

Winthrop Jordan argues that "Shakespeare used the theme of black and white sexuality in Othello, appealing to his society's taste in finding "Negro" men "peculiarly sexual." (38) Vogel's representation of Desdemona in an implicitly lesbian context also challenge such assumptions that Shakespeare's Othello has also been portrayed as a sexual object by decolonizing his black male body from indicators of any possible sexual oppression. Opposing Daniel Fischlin and Mark Fortier who in their very useful introduction to *Desdemona: A Play About a Handkerchief* criticize the play for its adaptive mode of neglecting the racial context of *Othello* (234), one can argue that the racial context of Othello is still a background reference in Vogel's play which celebrates counter-oppression by all means.

Published in a five years' interval, MacDonald's (1988) and Vogel's (1993) adaptations coincide a noteworthy period in the history of feminism, a period when the second wave feminist and the third wave feminist understandings started to coexist. The second wave feminism which was introduced in Europe, dominated the feminist movement, especially between 1960s and 1980s. Building on the first wave feminist (the 19th and early 20th centuries) understanding of women's suffrage and expanding it with a view to highlight the socio-political status of women, the second wave feminism is still the so-called mainstream feminism. The feminist theater critic Sharon Friedman notes, a great majority of feminist re-visions of the classics in theatrical form date back to the 1970s and after. As Friedman also reminds, such feminist revision inevitably introduces an experimental approach to earlier traditions of dramatic writing, performance and adaptation, usually being "subversive" (2–3)

Given the feminist context, both Vogel and MacDonald's adaptations can be considered to be what Teresa de Lauretis calls an "'oppositional appropriation' of dominant representation." (31) The two feminist playwrights both respond to Elaine Showalter's call for a truly female form, called "gynocriticism" in order to account for the female experience without the "linear" structures of the male tradition (131) and to Adrienne Rich's understanding of "feminist revision" which defines writing as an act of "renaming" (22): "We need to know the writings of the past, and know it differently than we have ever known it; not to pass on a tradition but break its hold over us." (19)

Vogel and MacDonald's subject matters deal with both the social and sexual contexts of women's bodily oppression. Approaching the third wave feminism in relation to the second wave feminism, it should be pointed out that "[m]any of the questions of third -wave feminism about the body, sexuality and femininity were similarly of concern to earlier generation"

(Eagleton and Parker 3) The third wave feminism which was introduced firstly in the States and right after in Canada, is usually read as a departure from the second wave feminism. While the major focus of the second wave feminism is, briefly, in the feminist writer Carol Hanisch's frequently quoted words "The personal is Political" (web), the "third wave feminism" which was coined by the American writer Rebecca Walker (39–41), emphasized the boundaries on the female body and was identified with women of color and lesbian feminisms. Another significant concern of the third wave feminism is the failure of feminism to account for the whole female experience, including race, class and sexuality, as the Chicana lesbian feminists Cherrie Moraga and Gloria Anzaldua assert in *This Bridge Called My Back: Writings of Radical Women of Color.* (x1iii–x1vii)

In other words, both plays echo the two feminist stances, justifying their own historical contexts, in transition between the two waves. Although Paula Vogel and Ann-Marie MacDonald's adaptations both deal with the white female body, which seems to stand outside the third wave feminist interest, their representations of the same sex female desire and the failure of 'female solidarity' among different groups of women, reinforce Moraga and Anzaldua's concern. Sharon Friedman contends that in Vogel's play "[t]he women use bodily presence and ribald language in place of whispering asides, delicately expressed confidences and plaintive ballads" (120) To exemplify, the Willow's song which Desdemona, unaware of Othello approaching, sings to Emilia in Act IV, Scene III is replaced by a conscious Desdemona counting the steps of Othello towards the chamber, in Vogel's play. Similarly, MacDonald's heroine Constance observes the rewriting of "indirect" and secret conversations to offer more direct and "active" dialogues, "questioning the fear of women's sexuality, the sexual desire that, plot-wise, leads to death, and the unexamined theme of love and power" (Fetterley xxiii–xxv) Constance's inner journey in meeting Desdemona and Juliet, which is no longer theoretical but observational, makes her recognize her authorial power and stand against Professor Knight. At the end of Act II, Desdemona and Juliet say "Happy Birthday Constance" which signifies Constance's rebirth.

Another innovation of Vogel and MacDonald is in representing women in various social roles and status, including the aristocrat, the servant, the whore, the intellectual, the wife and the lover, in order to offer possibilities of accommodating them together, in collaboration. In this respect, Vogel and MacDonald reinforce the post 1970s tradition of feminist theatre which aims at "feminist consciousness raising" as they break the "aesthetic distance" between the actors and audiences by drawing on 'the personal is political' principle. (Case 65, 66) Vogel's three female characters Desdemona, Emilia and Bianca finally find a room to reconcile their social identities in womanly unison. For instance, Vogel's Desdemona joins Bianca on Tuesdays in prostitution, which in turn breaks the oppositional representation of the two women as the aristocrat and the commoner. Unlike *Othello*'s Emilia, Emilia in *Desdemona: A Play About a Handkerchief* is sincere to Desdemona in telling, due to a misunderstanding, she gave the handkerchief to Iago. Thinking that "it's not safe" (253) for either of them, Desdemona and Emilia decide to depart together at the end of the play. In other words, Vogel links Desdemona to Emilia and Bianca, closely, and Emilia to Bianca, indirectly, through Desdemona, since they cannot bear one another. Similarly, MacDonald looks for ways of negotiation among her three female characters, Constance, Desdemona and Juliet. While she manages to unite Constance and Juliet in a feminist search, MacDonald loses Desdemona in internalized patriarchy. Constance's following address to Desdemona supports this idea: "[...] I must have been a monumental fool to think that I could save you from yourselves" (87)

Both Vogel and MacDonald offer a political stance in revisiting *Othello*, a play on woman's domestic victimization. In rewriting *Othello*, Vogel challenges to patriarchal restrictions of the society which finally victimize Desdemona, the very figure of an obedient wife. In her advice to Bianca, Vogel's Desdemona asserts that she is not *Othello*'s Desdemona: "[...] You don't have to care what anyone thinks about you- you're a totally free woman, able to snap your fingers in anyone's face." (246) As the above quotation indicates, Vogel's Desdemona challenges the stereotypical representation of an obedient woman, standing outside social conformism. Similarly, MacDonald resists the earlier representation of Desdemona as the victim or object of Othello's jealousy and reverses the plot, rewriting Desdemona as the jealous and revengeful subject. Constance's following lines support this idea: "Desdemona, I thought you were different; I thought you were my friend, I worshipped you. But you're just like Othello-gullible and violent." (86)

As Marianne Novy suggests, the two contemporary women playwrights are both very enthusiastic about closely examining Desdemona's transformation from an "adventurer" into "a victim" questioning the possibilities to prevent her tragedy. (67)

In the first act of the Shakespearean tragedy, Othello notes that "She [Desdemona] loved him for the dangers I [Othello] had pass'd [...]," wishing that "Heaven had made him such a man." (Act I, Scene III) In this respect, Desdemona has been given the potential to rebel in the Shakespearean text. However this potential was introduced at the exact time that it was suppressed, since the text situates Desdemona not as the storyteller but the listener. In the last act, Desdemona addresses Othello in fear, before Othello attempts to kill Desdemona in her chamber:

> And yet I fear you: for you are fatal then
> When your eyes roll so.
> Why I should fear, I know not,
> Since guiltiness I know not: But yet I feel I fear (Act V, Scene II)

As an obedient wife, however, she never attempts to escape and continues to call Othello, "my Lord" until death. This neglected potential of Desdemona in being the storyteller is what Paula Vogel and Ann-Marie MacDonald build on. In response to Desdemona's prayer to be "such a man," the two adaptations commonly make Desdemona such a woman: An adventurer, rather than a victim. Vogel carefully plays with the implications of Desdemona dying in bed and reads it not as a sign of domestic violence but that of female Desire, which is announced by her Desdemona as "[...] nothing will happen to me. I'm the sort that will die in bed." (239) Similarly, MacDonald's Desdemona, in jealousy, likens herself to an Amazon warrior. Her following lines put her adventuresome spirit forth:

> Did I not beat a path into the fray,
> my vow to honour in thy fool's cap quest?
> Did I not flee my father, here to dwell
> beneath the sword Hephaestus forged for Mars?
> Will I not dive into Sargasso Sea,
> to serve abreast the Amazons abroad?
> Will I not butcher any cow that dares
> low lies to call me tame, ay that I will!
> So raise I now the battle cry, *Bullshit!!* (38)

The idea of diving into Sargasso Sea can also be read as an explicit metaphor for an individual quest, which in turn reinforces the new image of Desdemona as an adventure-seeker. Now given humanly qualities such as jealousy, rivalry, curiosity and passion, the two Desdemonas become actively present in the text. In rewriting Desdemona in such a feminist context, Vogel and MacDonald effectively challenge the earlier representation of Desdemona as an instrument of Othello's jealousy, rivalry, curiosity and passion. In other words, both Vogel and MacDonald develop Othello's favorite object, Desdemona, as a female subject, recognizing her suppressed ideas, feelings and desire in a patriarchal environment. With the power of subversion and within the mode of adaptation, the two playwrights make their Desdemonas highly visible. As they freely adapt or appropriate the Shakespearean play by bringing into the play a feminist perspective, they respond to Adrienne Rich's feminist understanding of "revision[ing]." Vogel and MacDonald reinforce Rich by challenging the existing structures in *Othello* and reimagining destinies of women characters.

3 Black feminist *OTHELLOS*

Margaret Webster's 1943 production of *Othello* with a black actor -Paul Robeson- for the first time in the States is a significant phenomenon given the context of racial representations of Othello in the American continent. In its contemporary reception, the racial identity of Othello has become one of the most highlighted issues in the play, inevitably inspiring many productions. The black American actor William Marshall's several stage performances of Othello during the mid-20th century in Europe and America, stage and screen performances of Laurence Olivier in blackface, screen adaptations such as *Othello, the Black Commando* (1982) directed by Max H. Boulois starring Max H. Boulois and Tony Curtis and *Othello* (1995) directed by Olivier Parker starring Laurence Fishburne and Kenneth Branagh are among the noteworthy contemporary productions.

Representing Othello's race has always been a critical problem which led adapters to different choices such as shifting Othello and Iago's racial identities or performing Othello in blackface. 1604 November the first performance records of The King's Men, Shakespeare's theater company, shows that Othello was performed by a white actor in blackface in its London production. This tradition was visited in several later productions, including Laurence Olivier's stage and screen adaptations of *Othello*. Blackface minstrelsy implies the representation of a black character by a white actor either by wearing a black mask or by putting on dark make up. Contemporary perspectives foreground that such representations in turn distance the audiences from the reality of blackness and end up reflecting the white stereotypical connotations of blackness instead. As Paromita Chakravarti notes, "[t]he meaning of Othello, perhaps more so than other Shakespearean plays, depends on performance, the politics of performance and the politics surrounding the performance." (39) Given the context of blackface minstrelsy, which can be read as a political choice concerning the performance, the idea of a white actor playing Othello has inevitably problematized the performability of a black character, since such stage and screen adaptations have usually ended up representing a stereotype rather than offering a realistic representation of Othello as a black subject.

Another dilemma can be observed in terms of representing Othello either as a colored Asian or an African. As it is argued in *Shakespeare and Venice*, Othello has been situated as a "non-Muslim" African drawing on references of slavery, in the Middle East it has usually received as an Arab. (Holderness 46) Given this context one can recall an Egyptian adaptation of *Othello* as *At-Allah* or *Utayl* (1884) offering the first stage production of *Othello* in Arabic or a Turkish stage production of Othello as an Arabic Moor, *Arabın İntikamı* (1930s). These different interpretations of Othello in the West and Middle East interestingly refer to their own historical contexts and reflect both cultures' readings of the Other race. It is important to note that most productions in the American continent, such as the 1995 American screen adaptation of *Othello* (significant for being the first mainstream film production with a black actor – Laurence Fishburne – playing Othello), inevitably respond to Othello's blackness within the African-American context. Quite reinforced by recent postcolonial theories, contemporary adaptations of *Othello* in the American continent frequently attempt to represent the black identity of Othello without problematizing his blackness but problematizing the racist background instead. The before-mentioned Iqbal Khan's 2015 Royal Shakespeare Company production of Othello and Iago both as black characters, is also a noteworthy example of this recent trend.

The issue of race in *Othello*, however, is usually addressed by male adapters or producers whose primary concern has been representing Othello as a black male subject, decolonizing his body from white oppression. "Always, though, no matter how the character is cast, the body of Othello is racially marked." (Silverstone 78) Desdemona has been charmed by Othello's dark skin, which some critics read as a sign of Othello's commodification as an exotic object of white aristocratic woman's interest (Hodgson 46). Iago's villainy has been motivated by his feelings of inferiority as a white racist man, encountering a darker man's, Othello's power. In other words, Othello's race, inescapably, functions as a central signifier in the play. Drawing on the idea that Othello's body has been colonized by white subjects, postcolonial studies on *Othello* reinforce revolutionary representations of Othello's oppressed body, pointing out his body as the major sign of oppression in the play.

However, Othello's oppression of the white aristocratic lady Desdemona's body, has not yet become one of the favorite subjects of postcolonial critics, although postcolonial studies usually ally with feminism. According to black feminist theory, however, the black man considerably contributes to black woman's oppression by treating her as a reflection of his own degraded status in relation to white man and white woman. (Smith 123–127, hooks 7–76) The contemporary black feminist critic bell hooks theorizes that within the hierarchical scale, white woman is located above the black man. (16) In this respect, Shakespeare's Othello, as a black male subject, has already challenged the margins of the black theory centuries ago and this in turn situates the female issue in the play above that of race. As bell hooks further suggests, the less privileged group within this scale is, without any doubt, the black women (16), which Shakespeare's *Othello* leaves out. However, with a reference to Desdemona's mother's African maid who had died singing the Willow's Song, Shakespeare's *Othello* implies that Shakespeare, too, has thought about the black women (Act IV, Scene 2). Djanet Sears and Toni Morrison, two contemporary black women playwrights from the American continent, are distinguished for such women-centered representations of the African context in *Othello*. Following different adaptive methods, Sears and Morrison's adaptations of *Othello* improve the African context in the Shakespearean tragedy, from a postcolonial feminist gaze.

Born in 1959 in UK, Djanet Sears is a black Canadian playwright, actor and director who also teaches drama at the University of Toronto and the University College there. She was awarded multiple times in Canada for *Harlem Duet*. Being staged in New York in 2002 by a minor theater company and several times in Canada, the play failed to reach a global audience. Despite the significance of the contemporary debates it accommodates, the play still lacks the wide international recognition it deserves. Sears is also known for writing *Afrika Solo* (1987) and *The Adventures of a Black Girl in Search of God* (2001).

Sears's *Harlem Duet* is a prequel to *Othello* dramatizing Othello's choice to marry the white Desdemona, called Mona in Sears's play, after a love affair with a black girl called Billy in the city of Harlem. Sears's Othello is a black intellectual who is determined to start a relationship with his white colleague, conditioned to become visible in American society. Through this marriage and his new position as the coordinator of the department in Cyprus, Othello wishes to truly exist in the eyes of his colleagues, including

Chris Yago. At the very beginning, the play reminds the audience of the following lines by Othello before the prologue. In this respect, Sears's play not only announces its intention to centralize the issue of the handkerchief,

> ... That handkerchief
> Did an Egyptian to my mother give.
> She was a charmer...
> There's magic in the web of it.
> A sibyl... in her prophetic fury sewed the work. (Act III, Scene 4)

but also shows its desire to build on the Shakespearean play for the plot of which the handkerchief is very functional. Meeting the audience's expectations, the handkerchief is visited in the play multiple times. As Act 1 opens in 1928 Harlem, Billie reminds Othello of his mother's handkerchief which he gave Billie as a present. The dialogue is followed by their conversation on Harlem which Billie views as "the place to be now. Everyone who's anyone is coming here now. It's our time. In our place. It's what we've always dreamed of... isn't it?" (289); and thereby addresses the historical significance of Harlem, where black cultural movement of Harlem Renaissance occurs in the 1920s.

The above lines which follow the conversation on the handkerchief locate the Egyptian-made handkerchief at the center of race issue. Billie asks Othello if he loves Desdemona and whether she is white. Othello does not respond to her second question, and Billie takes the silence as yes/positive and tries to give the handkerchief back to Othello who refuses to take it. With a flashback to 1860 Harlem in Act 1 Scene 2, the readers/audiences witness Othello giving Billie the handkerchief which his mother gave him and their decision to get married and have children. Later in the play, full of revenge in hearing Othello and Mona's decision to get married, Billie uses the handkerchief as a tool for her black spell to ruin the new couple's lives. She pours a few drops of blood (that of her miscarriage, which she had kept in the fridge for all these years) onto the handkerchief and gives it to Othello. Reminiscent of Medea's pretended reconciliation scene with Jason and her sending with their children poisoned robes as a wedding present, Billie assures Othello that he needed to keep the handkerchief for his future children. As Othello refuses to take the handkerchief back, Billie asks Othello if he was not happy to receive his mother's handkerchief back, implying his indifferent attitude towards his African ancestry.

While the issue of race has always somehow been on the agenda of the American continent, Canada where Djanet Sears is from, is less central to the issue than the States and is also associated with an acknowledged British heritage through its Commonwealth ties. In Ric Knowles's interview, Djanet Sears puts it forth that race is not among Canada's major concerns: "Before Harlem Duet, Canadian Stage had never produced a work by an author of... African descent. And the problem with Canadian Stage is that it's called Canadian Stage, and it represents Canada, and I'm thinking, 'I'm Canadian, so it must represent me'" (Knowles 30). Djanet Sears incorporates the Canadian identity to her play, also metaphorically, with her innovative character called Canada. Canada, Billie's father, who in Act 2 comes to visit Billie and her brother's family, reflects a very reconciliating perspective towards the power relations in the household. In Buntin's interview, Sears notes that similar to the character Canada, Canada historically represents hope for slaves escaping from America. That in 2013 World Values Survey, Canada ranks among "the most race tolerant countries in the world," reinforces its perception as a more liberal place by the people of color. Billie and Othello's yearn for living in Canada where "freedom c[a]me" (294) before the States, also situates Canada as a liberal space for the black characters.

Within the time span of *Harlem Duet*, the country goes through two historically significant periods, namely, Emancipation and Harlem Renaissance, which signify difficult times for people of color. Although Othello considers himself "an American" (305), no longer "a minority" (305), he fails to reconcile with both American and African identities at once as his following lines put it forth: "If you don't hear my educated English, if you don't understand that I am a middle class educated man. I mean what does Africa have to do with me. We struttin' around professing some imaginary connection for a land we don't know. Never seen. Never gonna see." (305) Canada, on the other hand, keeps its welcoming position throughout the play and provides people of color a place where they are themselves, without "have[ing] to please no White folks no how." (302) Furthermore, the play ends with Canada embracing Billie, which signifies Canada's conciliatory presence as a neutral space for Billie's people. For further details on the play's reference to Canada, see Chapter 4, which discusses the Canadian writer Djanet Sears's dialogue with the canonical English writer Shakespeare within the context of Shakespeare and Canada.

The Pulitzer Prize and Nobel Prize winning American writer, editor, essayist and professor Toni Morrison was born in 1931, Ohio, as Chloe Ardelia Wofford. Her novels include *The Bluest Eye* (1970), *Sula* (1973), *Song of Solomon* (1977), *Tar Baby* (1981), *Beloved* (1987), *Jazz* (1992), *Paradise* (1997), *Love* (2003), *A Mercy* (2008) and *Home* (2012) Morrison has also published a short story called "Recitatif" (1983) and two plays, *Dreaming Emmett* (1986) and *Desdemona* (2011), besides a libretti, *Margaret Garner* (2005), many celebrated theoretical books and essays as well as books for children.

Toni Morrison's play *Desdemona* (2012) was first staged in collaboration with the Malian singer and songwriter Rokia Traore and the very well-known stage director Peter Sellars. The stage production received very positive criticism by the critics, "shin[ing] a new light on Shakespeare's tragedy." (La Croix) The play offers a postcolonial feminist appropriation of *Othello*, loosely following the plot of the source text. The play's main innovation is in representing an unrepresented character, Barbary, in the source text. "Barbary" which means Africa, is Desdemona's black maid who raised her. Peter Sellars notes that although Shakespeare did not write for Barbary, he imagined her. (8) However he points out that it is the major bias of Shakespeare's Othello to represent an "imagined Africa" and adds that the starting point of *Desdemona* was to challenge that. (7–11)

Through her emotional ties with Barbary, Morrison gives Desdemona an African background, foregrounding that she was raised by an African woman with all the folklore, songs as well as stories and thus justifies her emotional attachment to Othello. Thus, Morrison ensures that her representation of Desdemona foregrounds the black female experience as "migratory," a term used by Carole Boyle Davies to account for their existence in "myriad" times and spaces. (47)

> I exist in between, now: between being killed
> and being un-dead; between life on earth
> and life beyond it; between all time, which
> has no beginning and no end, and all space
> which is both a seedling as well as the sun it
> yearns for [...] (14)

The above lines by Morrison's Desdemona reassert that Shakespeare's Desdemona is a timeless and spaceless character, beyond past and present. The idea that Desdemona transcends timely and spatial representations also implies her perpetual adaptability. In other words, the lines above may also be considered as Morrison's justification of her writerly interest in reimagining Shakespeare's Desdemona.

While Sears's Desdemona, Mona, is referred to as a distinctly white aristocrat, Morrison's Desdemona is culturally "hybrid," borrowing from Homi K. Bhabha, at the crossroads between the colonizer and the colonized. Sears's Mona, a non-represented off-stage voice, is dethroned in the text by Billie. However Morrison's Desdemona is developed as the major character, being not only herself but also an extension of Barbary. In her first encounter with the audiences, Desdemona mentions that her parents gave her the name "Desdemona" which means misery and notes; "They were wrong. They knew the system, but they did not know me. I am not the meaning of a name I did not choose." (13) The above-mentioned quote reflects Morrison's Desdemona's resentment for her strict life provided by her own parents. The European sense of conformity is also implied, especially in the following words "They knew the system, but they did not know me." (13) As Desdemona's parents name her "Desdemona," they locate their own daughter within her tragic destiny. Given this context, Desdemona's biological parents, coming from a white aristocratic background, can be considered within the oppressive system. In this respect, Desdemona as a female child has also been oppressed by the system which precedes her individual choices.

On the other hand, "Barbary" whose name sounds similar to the English Word "barbarian" stands outside this system, with her unbound soul. In the following lines, Desdemona talks about Barbary, in fascination, as the most foregrounding figure in her childhood:

My solace in those early days lay with my
nurse, Barbary. She alone encouraged a slit
in that curtain. Barbary alone conspired with
me to let my imagination run free. She told
me stories of other lives, other countries.
Places where gods speak in thundering
silence and mimic human faces and forms.
When nature is not a crafted, pretty thing,
but wild, sacred and instructive. [...] (18)

Barbary is addressed as the source of Desdemona's childhood imagination, since she feeds Desdemona with various colors of her indigenous culture. Barbary grasps nature, unlike Desdemona's parents who are very culture centered. Barbary represents many aspects of the vivid African culture including the storytelling, blues and dance:

> She was more alive than anyone I knew
> and more moving. She tended
> me as though she were my birth mother:
> braided my hair, dressed me, comforted me
> when I was ill and danced with me when I
> recovered. I loved her. Her heart so wide,
> seemed to hold the entire world in awe and
> to savor its every delight (18)

Considering Barbary as her mother, Desdemona discovers both love and joy through her. Barbary's death is therefore recalled in the play, much later, as a traumatic incident in Desdemona's life. Barbary has left so deep traces in Desdemona that she is attracted to Othello because his looks resemble the way Barbary looked. Barbary, which means Africa, symbolizes Desdemona's emotional ties to Africa. Replacing the dead Barbary, Othello provides another access to African culture that fascinates Desdemona: "We danced together, our bodies moving in such harmony it was as though we had known each other all our lives." (23)

Morrison's treatment of Barbary not only as a character but also as a cultural reflection of Africa resembles Sears's representation of Canada both as a character and as a geographical space. Canada embraces all characters in the play; yet calls Billie in her Canadian name, "Sybill," which she dislikes. Desdemona likes Barbary too much; but calls her "Barbary," stereotyping her like the other white people. However, "Barbary" which means "Africa" and recalls the strong negative word "barbarian" in English, is not Desdemona's nurse, Saran's real name.

Another common point in the two adaptations is that unlike Shakespeare's Iago, their antagonists are not personified or individualized, but addressed, collectively, as racist ideology. In both adaptations, the protagonist Othello nearly serves as an instrument for the female subjects to enter the text easily. While in Morrison's text Othello nearly echoes Edwards Said's *Orientalism* by saying Desdemona "You never loved me. You fancied the idea of me, the exotic foreigner" (50), his point is later refuted by Desdemona "My mistake was believing that you hated war as much as I did. You believed I loved Othello the warrior. I did not. I was the empire you had already conquered." (54) Similarly Sears's Othello remains secondary to Billy in recognizing the soul of Harlem. For instance to his words on white feminism, Billie comments: "White wisdom from the mouth of the mythical Negro" (304), implying Othello's canonical position in relation to the Shakespearean text. The above line, in other words, can be considered as a direct intertextual reference to Shakespearean text which situates Othello as a legendary black character from the dominant white perspective. The black character Billie's above-mentioned critical awareness of Othello's internalization of white consciousness, despite his foregrounding African heritage, reminds the reader one of the early black theorists', Du Bois's, suggestion of "double consciousness" as the central characteristics of black identity. "Double consciousness" which Du Bois defines as "the sense of always looking at oneself through the eyes of the other" (2), is very much foregrounded in Billie's critical gaze directed at Othello, incorporating the black perspective towards being black and white perspective towards the black. Similarly in Morrison's *Desdemona*, Othello's following address to Desdemona involve "double consciousness": "I was doubted and deceived at every turn. Why? Because I was sold into slavery? Or because I was better than they? Whatever the reason, I had to prove myself over and over again." (53) Morrison's Othello puts it forth that he experiences a complicated search for identity since he cannot help viewing himself from his own perspective and the Other's perspective at the same time. Reminiscent of the contrastive sad and fast beats of blues revisited in stage performances of both adaptations, Du Bois's understanding of double consciousness incorporates the "veil" and "gift" of being black.

"Storytelling" and "rememory," two major features to characterize African-American literary tradition, are also among the common elements employed in Sears and Morrison's plays. While *Harlem Duet* tells the story of Othello's first wife Billie in relation to Harlem culture, *Desdemona* tells the story from the perspectives of the dead in their afterlives and reinforces the African belief that the dead still exist in myriad times and spaces. As Othello's mother, Soun, and Desdemona's mother, Madam Brabantio, encounter in the graveyard, Soun also mentions that they build an "altar" to the spirits waiting to console them. Given the context of rememory, *Harlem Duet* reminds the postcolonial feminist reader of an earlier text, a novel written by Dominica born "Creole" writer Jean Rhys, *Wide Sargasso Sea*, which tells the story of Mr. Rochester's "Creole" wife Bertha Mason before his marriage to *Jane Eyre*, the canonized heroine of English fiction. Similarly, Morrison's *Desdemona*'s treatment of rememory resembles that in Morrison's celebrated novel, *Beloved*, in which Sethe's dead baby daughter Beloved comes back to life to foreground her own story. In this respect, both postcolonial feminist appropriations of *Othello* revisit the postcolonial feminist tradition of writing besides the source text, Shakespeare's *Othello*.

Blackface minstrelsy, which has been mentioned earlier as a significant motive in African-American literature, should also be noted since it is very foregrounding in Sears's and Morrison's adaptive strategies. Traditionally, white performers used to imitate black race by wearing black mask or by putting on black make-up on their faces, which creates a distance between the actor's and the character's bodies. Constantin Stanislavsky's 1896 performance of Othello is especially noteworthy since although Stanislavski himself theorized that for the sake of a realistic representation the actor and the character should become one, his own performance of Othello in dark make up was received as "iconic" by most audiences and critics. This in turn points out the problem of representing an Other race and even displays the inadequacy of certain performance techniques. Black performers also responded to blackface minstrelsy by wearing dark black mask or by polishing their faces into pitch black so as to represent white performers' stereotypical representations of the black race. One can therefore argue that any blackface minstrelsy has historically implied a distanced, therefore stereotypical and unrealistic, representation of the black race. Early white representations of blackness often ended up with stereotyping, not necessarily because of prejudgments or preconditionings but also because of lack of access to direct information on the culture.

As Graham Holderness posits, the reality of Africa to Shakespeare still remains a mystery. Peter Sellars, the director of *Desdemona*, notes in his *Foreword* to the play that the major intention of their project was to represent a real Africa, not an "imagined" Africa as Shakespeare did. Sellars's words imply their reception of Shakespeare's representation of Africa and blackness as quite stereotypical, reminiscent of the tradition of blackface minstrelsy. In Buntin's interview, Djanet Sears mentions that she was inspired by Laurence Olivier's performance of *Othello* in blackface which disturbed her (web). Sears further points out that she was motivated to represent Othello from her own perspective and indirectly announces her adaptive strategy as a reverse minstrelsy. There are direct references to minstrel mask in the play which also supports this idea. For instance one of their conversations, Billie calls Othello who calls himself "an actor," "[a] minstrel. A black minstrel." (312) While packing Othello's properties Billie finds a mask and gives it to the landlady, Magi, to keep for her. As Othello visits Billie to take his belongings, he steps on a piece of the broken mask, examines it and puts it on the mantel. (304) In the same scenes where the mask or minstrelsy are reminded, there are important discussions on black man and white society as well as black man in relation to black woman. Given this context, the mask signifies Othello's role in the white society he chooses over Harlem.

In this respect, one can trace the black cultural heritage in both writers' conceptions of the race issue. Storytelling, rememory, blues, black magic juxtaposed with blackface minstrelsy in the two adaptations serve as tools for remythologizing the black context in Shakespeare's *Othello*. Margaret Jane Kidnie metaphorically reads Djanet Sears's adaptation as a means of "exorcizing the past," which by building on *Othello*, a canonical work and a symbol of blackface tradition, intends to haunt "a theatrical 'ghost.'" (71) While *Harlem Duet* challenges the tradition of representation on one layer, on another layer it situates myths as old collective stories definitely telling the past, but not necessarily the present.

In Mat Buntin's interview, Djanet Sears notes "…when adapting Shakespeare, we are really trying to break away from our foundational mythologies by revisioning them and in so doing we create a new covenant, a new testament. […], I think it is part of an attempt to have a relationship and yet distance ourselves from our mythological traditions and our forbearers in order to be individual." (web) Reinforcing her adaptive strategies, Sears offers Othello and Billie in a dialogue while sharing their books, among which Shakespeare's name is mentioned besides African Mythology. Given this context, one can argue whether Sears intends to "revise" the mainstream mythologies by juxtaposing them with less known ones. Djanet Sears's and Toni Morrison's intentional intertextual relations with Shakespeare's

Othello and one another can be traced to the well-known critic Henri Louis Gates's notion of black semiotics, an everlasting "signif[ication] upon" a previous text. What Gates calls "Signifyin(g) on" in his celebrated work *"The Signifying Monkey: A Theory of Afro-American Literary Criticism,* involves both repetition and alteration of an already written text and serves as a "metaphor for formal revision, or intertextuality, within the Afro-American literary tradition." (261) Drawing on Gates's understanding of signification, one can suggest that as the major signifier of racial representations in the white canon, Shakespeare's *Othello* provides an open-ended tool for a possible black revision. In this respect, Morrison's play "signif[ies] upon" Sears's play while the two works "signify upon" the racial context of Shakespeare's *Othello*. In other words, the two black appropriations foreground *Othello* as a possible space for an everlasting adaptive process, making a call for new black *Othellos*.

Djanet Sears's treatment of black man and black woman relations echoes the black feminist theorist bell hooks who suggests the oppression by black man finally places black women at the very bottom, with an "overall status lower than that of any other group" (2000:16) while the question Billie poses "Ain't I a woman" reminds the postcolonial readers the words of an earlier black feminist theorist, Sojourner Truth. (web) Black feminism has also argued that white mainstream feminism fails to reflect the black women's situation. (bell hooks, 1989:182) Djanet Sears reverses this attitude in not representing Mona as a developed character and leaving her as an off-stage voice, and even a stereotype for white female intellectual. From the perspective of Billie, Mona is commodified as white female flesh: "Here, before me – his woman – all blonde hair and blonde legs. Her weight against his chest. His arm around her shoulders, his thumb resting on the gold of his hair." (296) Billie addresses Mona as "his woman" as if Mona is Othello's object. As the above lines indicate, Billie's gaze towards Mona is also very much exclusive and race-centered. Female solidarity, however, is very much foregrounded in Harlem where Billie is usually accompanied by two other black women, Magi and Amah. Jennie, Billie's niece, also functions within female solidarity, as if their mutual daughter, their common hope for future. In this respect, Sears's understanding of feminism in *Harlem Duet* is a black feminism rather than a unifying feminism.

The representation of black man and black woman relationships in Sears's play also reinforces the black feminist perspective which suggests that black women also suffer from black men. (hooks 16, 17) To exemplify, Billie's relationship with Othello implies a series of self-sacrifice. Billie is left by Othello with unkept promises, having an abortion and a miscarriage in the background. Although in the past she gave her inheritance from her parents to Othello's school, favoring his education over her own, Othello later refuses to pay for her single course. As in the following lines Othello accuses black women for being unable to overcome their traumatic pasts, he displays his preconditionings towards black women: "To a black woman, I represent every Black man she has ever been with and with whom there was still so much to work out." (305)

Toni Morrison's adaptation also reflects the playwright's sensitive concern for black man and black woman issue which she had earlier employed in many of her novels including *Beloved* and *Sula*. In her only short story published, *Recitatif*, Morrison also highlights the race issue from the juxtaposed gazes of one black and one white woman. In *Desdemona*, Toni Morrison looks for a more reconciling ground for black and white women, giving Desdemona an African connection. However, Morrison makes sure that she does not undermine the difficulty in this process by writing Barbary and Desdemona in the following conversation:

> Desdemona: Barbary! Barbary! Come closer. How I have
> missed you. Remember the days spent by the
> canal? We ate sweets and you saved the honey
> for me eating none yourself. We shared so much.
> Barbary: We shared nothing.
> Desdemona: What do you mean?
> Barbary: I mean you don't even know my name.
> Barbary? Barbary is what they call Africa.
> Barbary is the geography of the foreigner,
> the savage. Barbary? Barbary equals the
> sly, vicious enemy who must be put down
> at any price; held down at any cost for the
> conquerors' pleasure. Barbary is the name of
> those without whom you could never live
> nor prosper. (45)

As Desdemona says she had known her all her life, Barbary puts it forth more directly as "I am black-skinned. You are white-skinned." (45) However,

Morrison makes Desdemona underline their shared destiny as "Sa'ran. We are women. I had no more control over my life than you had. My prison was unlike yours but it was a prison still." (48) Toni Morrison's unifying feminist concern is different than Djanet Sears's understanding of black-centered feminism. Morrison's feminist concern sometimes prevails over the racial content of *Desdemona*, as the black Othello finally apologizes to white Desdemona and confesses that he killed Desdemona and himself "to stop the drama." (54) While Morrison's Othello is depicted as a power-centered or even an oppressive figure, her Desdemona signifies tolerance and peace as well as the end of colonialism, which is asserted in her following lines: "My mistake was believing that you hated war as much as I did. You believed I loved Othello the warrior. I did not. I was the empire you had already conquered. Alone together we could have been invincible." (54) Rokia Traore's final song *Kele Mandi* incorporated into *Desdemona*, also reinforces the conciliatory ground of the play:

> When two beings meet,
> each brings to the other a bit of themselves.
> So we learn, we construct our selves, we evolve.
> I bring what makes me different from you.

As learning is underlined above as a considerable part of the socially constructed identities, the issue of "difference" is located on a dynamic axis. The interchanging use of personal references such as 'I' and 'you', 'self' and 'other' also reflect the arbitrariness of codes and stereotypes:

> Give me a bit of what you are.
> But do it with gentleness and tolerance,
> since all that you impose upon me with force
> will only leave the imprint
> of your violence and your arrogance.

While sincere communication is addressed as the only possible solution, Traore's song makes a call for further empathy on both parts:

> One can't force the other
> to accept what is offered.
> In accepting what you have to give,
> I open you to what I have to offer. (55)

The above lines reinforce the confrontation between different subjects, de-polarizing the racial difference through hybridization. Asking the other to give a bit of himself, the lyrics of Traore's song reinforces Homi K. Bhabha's before-mentioned conception of "hybridity" as a source of mutual tolerance. As Traore's song challenges the binary opposites "one" and "the other," it makes a call for a true reconciliation.

As for Sears's play, the racial distinctions are so centered to call the play culturally black. For instance the scene where Billie thought she was looking at Mona's white legs through Othello's gaze, places the issue of race before the feminist content. Sears juxtaposes her Black heroine with both Othello and Mona, her *Harlem Duet* with Shakespeare's *Othello*, in an urge to write an African *Othello*, in a loose dialogue with Shakespeare. *Desdemona*'s major innovation is in involving music and African oral tradition in order to refigure the play with an African background. While Sears's appropriation "signif[ies] on *Othello*, Morrison's adaptation signifies on Sears' adaptation as well. Morrison's addition of black oral tradition into a white canonical text goes parallel to her use of an ever "signify[ing]" language, in the above-mentioned sense which Henry Louis Gates suggests. The generic characteristics of drama, which is a considerably new way of writing for Morrison, inevitably points out a potential of everlasting signification, owing to its performativity. However, black semiotic consciousness has obviously contributed to the style which makes it more visible.

Distinguishing adaptive strategies of the two contemporary women black playwrights are also reflected in their choices of titles. Toni Morrison's title, *Desdemona,* initially implies that the play intends to offer a female-centric perspective on *Othello*. As Morrison's title foregrounds one of Shakespeare's characters, it also provides a remarkable reference to Shakespeare. Sears's play *Harlem Duet*, however, foregrounds Harlem in a way to deground *Othello*. Its title announces the adaptive strategy of juxtaposition with its reference to 'duet', a double-voiced singing, probably standing as a metaphor for Othello and Billie's relationship.

From a comparative perspective, Sears's representation of nonlinear plot which breaks the conventional plotline can be considered more revolutionary while Morrison's *Desdemona* can be considered milder in tone and less experimental in form, comparatively. Dwelling on a more subversive layer, Sears loosely adapts or appropriates *Othello* by Shakespeare and makes sure to avoid any Shakespearean markers in her black play, *Harlem Duet*.

Morrison, on the other hand, acknowledges her dialogue with Shakespeare by calling her adaptation, simply *Desdemona*. Sears and Morrison's writerly dialogues with Shakespeare will be further discussed in the next chapter, together with those of MacDonald and Vogel.

4 Conclusion: writerly dialogues and adaptive strategies: authorship or authority?

As discussed in earlier chapters, *Othello* inevitably represents a racist and misogynist society. However, it is quite noteworthy to distinguish between the values of his society that Shakespeare represents and the world he idealizes. Where Shakespeare personally stands in *Othello* can better be assessed by reading into his writerly strategy: "Shakespeare plays with us throughout Othello, exploiting stereotypes, arousing expectations, alternately fulfilling and frustrating our preconceptions." (Vaughan 69) Shakespearean catharsis operates with an aim to make the audiences realize the tragic consequences of extreme social implications on human life. Racism and misogyny are the exemplified themes of social oppression, the presence of which is never praised but indirectly judged. Contemporary female responses to *Othello* should then better be received within the context of responding to the content Shakespeare represents in *Othello* as well as what Shakespeare represents as an icon. The personal Shakespeare will therefore be left outside this discussion.

Julie Sanders argues that women writers' adaptive dialogues with Shakespeare usually show the characteristics of an appropriation: "By adapting Shakespeare, women writers self-consciously range themselves either within or alongside the Academy, in an often tense, occasionally directly resistant relationship." (4) However, based on the earlier-provided comparative analysis of contemporary adaptations of *Othello*, it should be noted that while the Canadian playwrights Ann-Marie MacDonald and Djanet Sears choose to dethrone Desdemona juxtaposing her with alternative female characters, the American writers Paula Vogel and Toni Morrison named their plays after "Desdemona." While the four plays commonly offer feminist adaptations of *Othello*, MacDonald and Sears's adaptations demonstrate comparatively loose dialogues with the source text, respectively parodying and precursing the Shakespearean play. Vogel and Morrison, on the other hand, choose to work on certain parts of Othello by offering a prequel and a postquel, respectively.

Ann-Marie MacDonald's comic rewrite titled *Goodnight Desdemona, Good Morning Juliet* (1988) addresses the feminist literary critic's struggle to read the two tragedies by Shakespeare against a patriarchal content. However, as its title announces, MacDonald makes an adaptive choice of incorporating the two tragedies, *Othello* and *Romeo and Juliet*, within her play, and juxtaposing the two female characters as they go through a feminist test. The heroine Constance, looking for the missing comic element in the Gustav manuscript, finally realizes that the writer is the wise fool which in turn is she herself. Constance's intellectual background which in turn leads to a critical perspective on *Othello* turns the tragedy into the comedy she was looking for, when added to her personal ignorance and lack of insight.

Constance's critical stance which places her as an outsider in the text, in turn, reflects on the adaptive status of MacDonald's play which is a self-reflexive and intergeneric appropriation of *Othello* while it also foregrounds MacDonald's authorial dialogue with Shakespeare on the idea of adapting. Constance's following lines imply that her involvement in the play as a critical reader also puts her in a writerly status: "I merely must determine authorship. But have I permanently changed the text?" (33) However, given the context of postmodern parody, she soon realizes that she can hardly talk about authority:

> [...] In that case, I've preempted the Wise Fool!
> He must be here somewhere- I'll track him down
> and reinstate him in the text,
> and then I'll know who wrote this travesty,
> since every scholar worth her salt agrees,
> the Fool is the mouthpiece of the Author! (33)

Constance's lines, with a self-reflexive technique, refer to the form of the play as "travesty," which in turn reflects the play's in-between situation. However readers soon realize that the mode of comedy is more dominant as Constance utters the last line of the above quote: "the Fool is the mouthpiece of the Author!" (33) In other words, as Constance realizes, in a postmodern work such as this travesty, the writer is doomed to be the fool rather than a figure of authority. In this respect, one can recall the scene in which Constance is represented in the graveyard: "Then I was right about your plays. They were comedies after all, not tragedies. I was wrong about one thing, though: I thought only a Wise Fool could turn tragedy to comedy." (87) As the ghost laughs, Constance remembers Yorick in *Hamlet* and realizes she was the Fool and the Author since they "are the one and the same" while the Ghost calls her a beardless bard, implying a female Shakespeare (87).

Hence, it is implied that Constance is MacDonald's mouthpiece, the image of the fool, which she was theoretically convinced to be the source of this travesty, by changing the tragedy into a comedy. These lines also reflect on MacDonald's authorial dialogue with Shakespeare by signifying the genre transformative, hybrid adaptive process itself. On the authorial layer, MacDonald is the writer who changes the Shakespearean tragedy into a comedy by introducing Constance, the contemporary female scholar and making her pretend as the Fool. Although in a mock serious content MacDonald does address the Bard, her authorly dialogue with Shakespeare can still be viewed as serious. As Constance's pen finally turns into gold and it is the Chorus telling this legendary incident, MacDonald probably asks for a praise for being a gifted writer and reminds the readers and audiences of the source of the Fool as Greek mythologies, not Shakespeare.

Another noteworthy strategy is that MacDonald's play finally asserts Desdemona as a feminine figure having internalized patriarchy and foregrounds Juliet as a lesbian feminist character. In this respect, MacDonald's mock serious treatment to *Othello* possibly serves to an instrumental purpose to centralize *Romeo and Juliet*. Incorporating the two well-known tragedies by Shakespeare with a postmodern feminist consciousness besides a mock serious attitude is the major innovation in MacDonald's adaptive strategy. Saying "I was being mischievous by using Shakespeare as a source in the same way he used everyone else as a source" (141), in Rita Much's interview, MacDonald underlines her conscious contemporary feminist dialogue with the Bard, revealing her mock serious tone as an adaptive strategy. Mark Fortier addresses MacDonald's feminism as the underlying motivation in adapting Shakespeare as "if Shakespeare were a woman, with a woman's experience" (51) and thus accounts for MacDonald's subversive dialogue with the Shakespearean source texts as a feminist reversal.

Djanet Sears's black feminist rendering of *Othello* and *Harlem Duet* manifests its adaptive strategy towards writing a prequel to Shakespeare's play, foregrounding Othello's previous lover Billie, a black intellectual, dethroning Desdemona or Mona, as the play addresses her. The critic Margaret Kidnie reads Sears's writerly motivation as to "exorcise the past" (71) and her strong wish to resist the Shakespearean text functions in the form of a juxtaposition between her innovated black female protagonist and Othello. Similarly Ric Knowles reads Sears's motivation in *Harlem Duet* as "exorciz[ing] Othello" and views Sears's adaptive style as a loose dialogue with Shakespeare, suggesting that *Harlem Duet* requires no specific knowledge on the Shakespearean source text but some affinity with Desdemona, Othello and Iago. (158) The Canadian playwright Djanet Sears offers a black Canadian *Othello*, celebrating neither of the Shakespearean protagonists, the black Othello or the white Desdemona, but her own innovation, Billie, a black feminist intellectual. As Sears announces in the opening of her play, *Harlem Duet* is a "rhapsodic blues tragedy," belonging more to Harlem than Shakespeare. The play therefore asserts its status as a black feminist play and a loose adaptation. Using authorial references to Shakespeare in Billie and Othello's dialogues while they were sharing their library books and drawing on a linguistic allusion in naming its characters Mona and Yago, while keeping Shakespeare's protagonist Othello as Othello, Sears's play provides an alternative *Othello*. As Sears minimizes the role of Othello in her own play, Sears's text announces its intention to dethrone its source text.

In *Harlem Duet*, Sears also provides a black Canadian appropriation of Shakespeare's *Othello* with a distinctively feminist consciousness. Her involvement of the Canadian context is also metaphorically reflected onto one of its characters, Canada, who is Billie's father. Canada in the play stands for the reconciliation between past and present and therefore reflects on Sears's adaptive strategy in revisiting the Shakespearean tragedy with a postcolonial feminist perspective. Given this context, the question one of the characters ask Canada in *Harlem Duet,* "Canada, where do you get these ideas of Harlem from?", even sounds from Shakespeare addressing the adapter, Sears.

Ric Knowles comparatively studies the two Canadian playwrights MacDonald and Sears's innovations in "Shakespeare in Canada" context. He praises MacDonald's "generic revisioning" and reads Sears's appropriation as a manifestation of a "high cultural hybridity" which respectively "asserts, reclaims, and undermines canonical cultural authority." (163) In this respect, Knowles underlines the hybrid characteristics of Canadian cultural identity, which connects intergeneric and intertextual adaptive strategies of MacDonald and the in-between spatial and timely representations of Sears. Shakespeare in Canada is a very significant context since being a Commonwealth country, they show loyalty to their European pasts, still viewing Shakespeare as a part of their collective backgrounds as well as their cultural identities. On the other hand, they are conscious of being a part of the American Continent, away from Europe. It is very interesting to note that Canadian culture itself is hybrid and the genre of adaptation which is technically hybrid has its theoretical rise inevitably there. The following lines by Knowles effectively put the major dilemma of "Shakespeare in Canada" project forth as authorizing or de-authorizing Shakespeare:

> It may be that adapting Shakespeare risks reinscribing his cultural
> Author-ity, but that authority permeates Canadian culture willynilly.
> It may be also that 'taking on'-challenging, appropriating, and
> disarticulating- that authority, [...], Canadian cultural values and
> Canadian gendered, racial, ethnic and classed subjectivities have
> been productively renegotiated in cultural productions [...] in the last
> three decades of the 20th century. (164)

The two American women playwrights Paula Vogel and Toni Morrison's adaptations deal with *Othello,* without directly referring to Shakespeare. While MacDonald refers to William Shakespeare with an intertextual consciousness, Sears's Othello and Billie mention Shakespeare while sharing their library books. However, the name Shakespeare never appears either in *Desdemona: A Play About a Handkerchief* or in *Desdemona.*

As for Paula Vogel's *Desdemona; A Play About a Handkerchief,* which was examined as a lesbian feminist appropriation of *Othello,* the main focus is on a set of conversations in the ladies' chamber. Vogel's play leaves out the male characters and reduces Shakespeare's protagonist, Othello, to a background voice while she recenters Emilia and Bianca, together with her lesbian Desdemona within the female solidarity which feminism has been yearning for.

Vogel's adaptation differs from those of MacDonald and Sears as it draws on a more specific part of *Othello,* the scene in ladies' chamber in Act 4, which centralizes the issue of handkerchief. Its specificity in its dialogue with the source text inevitably announces a comparatively closer reading of *Othello.* The level of subversion in adaptations are quite often manifested in the choice of titles, usually reflective of the adapter's perspective. Vogel's title also implies a focus on the female protagonist Desdemona, in relation to the handkerchief, which reinforces the reader's expectations for a highly feminist content underneath a mock serious treatment.

To meet its readers' expectations, *Desdemona: A Play About a Handkerchief* leaves Othello, Iago and Cassio, the three odd men of *Othello*, out. While silencing male characters of *Othello*, allocating their powers of speech to Desdemona, Emilia and Bianca, Vogel offers a thorough feminist version of the Shakespearean play. Vogel's feminist concern is also manifested in breaking the hierarchical distinction between Shakespeare's female characters by including Bianca within the female solidarity as represented by ladies' chamber. While Shakespeare's Bianca is a whore and Desdemona is a lady of virtue, Vogel challenges the female characterization in the source text to a point to blur the conventional understandings of virtue and whoredom. Accepting Bianca to ladies' chamber, a place where sisterhood fails in the Shakespearean text and recentering it as a potential space for female bondage, Vogel reinforces the strength of her own content, as announced in her choice of the title. With their submissive representations in Shakespeare's *Othello*, it is Bianca and Emilia, indeed, who enable the male characters' intrusion in women's private sphere. The handkerchief, in this respect, symbolizes the failure of women in defending their jeopardized space under patriarchy.

Since Vogel's adaptive strategy operates initially through a deconstruction of the Shakespearean characterization of a passive, girlish Desdemona and finally a reconstruction of her as an active woman, her dialogue with the Shakespearean text grows looser throughout the play. As Vogel chooses not to change the final plot, making Desdemona die, she takes the benefit of pointing out the patriarchal content of *Othello* in a more effective way. To put it forth in Jennifer Flaherty's words, "[b]y appropriating Desdemona from Shakespeare's text, Vogel can 'give back to Desdemona power to accompany her activity' (Jardine 34) if she so chooses. Yet instead of rewriting the plot of Othello to give Desdemona a stronger voice, Vogel chooses to emphasize the social order which challenges Desdemona to act as a subject." In this respect, Vogel's adaptation can be called a feminist appropriation of *Othello*, quite subversive in content and strategically loyal in structure.

The structural fidelity to Shakespeare's *Othello* implies limited tension in authorial dialogue with the source text writer, Shakespeare or indicates, in Bloom's words, less "anxiety of Shakespearean influence." (xviii) In Harold Bloom's later psychoanalytical reading, Shakespeare is, subconsciously, an indispensable rival for the new generation creative writer "The largest truth of literary influence is that it is an irresistible anxiety. Shakespeare will never allow you to bury him, or escape him, or replace him. We have almost all of us, thoroughly internalized the power of Shakespeare's plays, frequently without having attended them or read them." (xviii)

The three above-mentioned adaptations can commonly be considered as contemporary feminist remakes or appropriations of *Othello*. In her comprehensive study titled *The Feminist Playwright as Critic*, Sharon Friedman notes that experimentation with time, space, language and body usually signals a conscious transposition. (114) Vogel, MacDonald and Sears commonly shift more than two of these elements which in turn implies a deliberate transformation. Friedman also suggests that Vogel, MacDonald and Sears's adaptations "play freely with Shakespeare's Othello to stage a counter universe [...]." (113)

This universe these three playwrights portray is reactively inspired by Shakespeare's *Othello* and does not intend to "look back" to Shakespeare's universe with "fresh eyes" (Rich 18) but rather make Shakespeare look into their new universe in regret. In this respect, these three plays cannot fully be considered "revision[ings]" of the Shakespearean tragedy *Othello*, in the sense that Adrienne Rich addresses in her seminal essay, "When We Dead Awaken: Writing As Revision." There Rich defines the term as "the act of looking back, of seeing with fresh eyes, of entering an old text from a new critical direction – is for woman more than a chapter in cultural history: it is an act of survival." (18). Given this context, women writers are invited by Rich to rewrite the classics with a feminist perspective, in order to refill their own missing spaces in the past. However according to Rich, such reinvention may be possible and effective only through a close dialogue with the preceding text. Furthermore, Adrienne Rich underlines the fact that an anxious dialogue with canonical writers as Shakespeare should be overcome if a real feminist perspective is to be offered:

> I think we need to go through that anger, and we will betray our own reality, if we try, as Virginia Woolf was trying, for an objectivity, a detachment, that would make us sound... more like Shakespeare. (48–49)

As Erickson notes, Rich's understanding of 're-vision' goes much beyond earlier feminists such as Virginia Woolf and is critical of Woolf for her "problematic accommodation with literary tradition" (165), as signified by Shakespeare. In her essay on MacDonald, Sears and Vogel's *Othellos*, Sharon Friedman observes that incorporating contemporary literary and performance theories as well as cultural studies, the three playwrights act as feminist critics "resist[ing], revise[ing] and produce[ing] new meanings in their dialogue with the Bard," together with the whole institutions serving the canon. (113, 114) However, such resistive approach inevitably gets caught on the layer of what Harold Bloom would call "the anxiety of [Shakespearean] influence" (xviii) The women writers who intend to revise Shakespeare would finally end up reasserting his power, recentering Shakespeare as a figure of literary authority.

Toni Morrison's *Desdemona* is the only play within the female canon of appropriations or loose adaptations of Othello examined here, which keeps its dialogue with the source text throughout the text and overcomes any writerly 'anxiety' or any personal 'anger' for the source text writer. Morrison's distinctive attitude is reflected in representing both Othello and Desdemona without juxtaposing them with alternative characters or an alternative plot. Morrison's play offers a close dialogue with Shakespeare's *Othello,* building on the Willow Song in Act IV where Desdemona tells Emilia about her mother's African maid Barbary, who died of a sorrowful love. In this respect, Morrison's play which writes in accordance with the Shakespearean plot, may not be considered an appropriation: "a decisive journey away from the source text" (Sanders 27), also Morrison and canon quote unlike Vogel, Sears and MacDonald's adaptations. As Peter Erickson who also calls *Desdemona* a 're-vision', notes, "What is more striking about Toni Morrison's engagement with Shakespeare is the extent to which her interpretation of Othello is grounded in close reading of Shakespeare's play." (1) The level of dialogue with the source text may better be judged according to the possibility of leaving the source text out in the process of reading. For instance, the reader of *Desdemona* would hardly survive without a pre-knowledge on *Othello*. This idea in turn foregrounds Toni

Morrison as an enthusiastic reader of Shakespeare and can be supported with the biographical fact that Morrison first intended to write her dissertation on Shakespeare, an intention which failed only because her supervisor did not approve her subject.

Adding to Shakespearean *Othello*, Morrison, in *Desdemona*, makes an adaptive choice towards truly representing Barbary, Desdemona's black nurse which Shakespearean *Othello* also mentioned but left out to develop. Through Barbary, Morrison also accounts for Desdemona's love for Othello and strengthens the underlying African context of the play, making it more visible. Through her emotional ties with Barbary, Desdemona is also given an African background, foregrounding that she was raised by an African woman with all the folklore, songs as well as stories and thus justifies her emotional attachment to Othello. Thus Morrison ensures that her representation of Desdemona foregrounds the black female experience as "migratory," a term used by Carole Boyle Davies to account for their existence in "myriad" times and spaces. (47)

> I exist in between, now: between being killed
> and being un-dead; between life on earth
> and life beyond it; between all time, which
> has no beginning and no end, and all space
> which is both a seedling as well as the sun it
> yearns for [...] (14)

The above lines by Morrison's Desdemona reassert that Shakespeare's Desdemona is a timeless and spaceless character, beyond past and present. The idea that Desdemona transcends timely and spatial representations also implies her perpetual adaptability. In other words, the above lines may also be considered as Morrison's justification of her writerly interest in reimagining Shakespeare's Desdemona in an after-life. In this respect, these lines also reflect on the notion of intertextual dialogue, asserting that a dead character in one text may still be alive in a second text, which inevitably indicates both a second space and a second time.

Morrison creatively treats Barbary not only as a character but also as a cultural reflection of Africa on the Western context. Morrison's Desdemona likes Barbary too much; but cannot help calling her nurse "Barbary," stereotyping her like the other white people. Morrison adds a new critical dimension in announcing that "Barbary" which means "Africa" and recalls the strong negative word "barbarian" in English, is not Desdemona's nurse's real name. Building on the canonical English writer Shakespeare's character, but differing from it "creatively" by offering an "interpretive" reading, and thus reinforcing Linda Hutcheon's suggestions for a good adaptation (8), Morrison renames her outside the white-centered perspective of the canonical play but within the African context of her own play as Saran.

Rokia Traore's final song Kele Mandi, incorporated into Desdemona, also reinforces the conciliatory ground of the play which Morrison underlines:

> When two beings meet,
> each brings to the other a bit of themselves.
> So we learn, we construct our selves, we evolve.
> I bring what makes me different from you.

The distinction between self and Other is further challenged in the below lines which make a call for unison by making what is distinctively 'mine', 'yours'.

> Give me a bit of what you are.
> But do it with gentleness and tolerance,
> since all that you impose upon me with force
> will only leave the imprint
> of your violence and your arrogance.

'Tolerance' is addressed as the major instrument to start a mild dialogue, while 'to accept' is softly underlined, within the margins of free will, as a necessary step for a mutual understanding.

> One can't force the other
> to accept what is offered.
> In accepting what you have to give,
> I open you to what I have to offer. (55)

The above lines reinforce the confrontation between different subjects, depolarizing the racial difference through hybridization. Asking the other to give a bit of himself, the lyrics of Traore's song reinforces Homi K. Bhabha's before-mentioned conception of "hybridity" as a source of mutual tolerance. As Traore's song challenges the binary opposites "one" and "the Other," it makes a call for a true reconciliation.

Graham Holderness suggests that the reality of Africa to Shakespeare still remains a mystery. One of Desdemona's major innovations is in refiguring the play within Shakespeare's imagination rather than writing an African play. Similarly Morrison's unifying sense of feminism operates not across but together with the Shakespearean text and therefore goes even a step further than a feminist re-visioning and dwells on a new path which might better be called a postfeminist re-visioning.

Toni Morrison's intentional intertextual relations with the source text and its preceding postcolonial and feminist adaptations can be better traced to the well-known critic Henri Louis Gates's notion of black semiotics, an everlasting "signif[ication]y upon" a previous text. What Gates calls "Signifyin(g) on" in his celebrated work *The Signifying Monkey: A Theory of Afro-American Literary Criticism*, involves both repetition and alteration of an already written text and serves as a "metaphor for formal revision, or intertextuality, within the Afro-American literary tradition." (261) Drawing on Gates's understanding of signification, one can suggest that as the major signifier of racial representations in the white canon, Shakespeare's *Othello* provides an open-ended tool for a possible black revision. As Morrison's *Desdemona*, "continuously revise[s]" and "alter[s]," therefore "signif[ies] on" *Othello* and its previous receptions, it reinforces Gates's suggestion of black semiotics. (xv–xx) In other words, Morrison's *Desdemona* "signif[ies] upon" both earlier adaptations and the engendered racial context of Shakespeare's Othello, with a black technique of revision, foregrounding Othello as a possible space for an everlasting adaptive process.

"Shakespeare is here, now, always what is currently been made out of him." (Holderness xvii) The above lines by Graham Holderness are taken from his celebrated work where he addresses Shakespeare as a 'myth'. (xvii) As Holderness puts forth, Shakespeare has become a sign, a collective figure which transcends over space and time. The more Shakespeare is 'myth[ified],' the less important he becomes as a person. To quote J. Hillis Miller, "There is not [or no more] any 'Shakespeare himself.' 'Shakespeare' is an effect of the text, which depersonalizes, disunifies." (59) In other words, it is more receptions of Shakespeare and his writing, rather than William Shakespeare himself, which has located the playwright on a mythical layer.

The feminist response to Shakespeare is actually a reaction to the male standards of Western literature, embodied in the idea of Shakespeare as an icon. As Susan Bassnet-McGuire suggests: "If the notion of linearity, of overview, is taken as a starting point for the theatre that is seen to be inherently male, then a specifically women's theatre may well be a theatre in search of a form." (463) Searching for an alternative form, although it takes place on different layers, is what these four playwrights share in common. While Ann-Marie MacDonald parodies the present form by juxtaposing the two tragedies and finally turning them into a comic play, Djanet Sears reverses the form into a nonlinear plot, exploring multiple times and spaces. Paula Vogel writes a prequel to *Othello* focusing on one single scene while Morrison represents alternative times and spaces by showing the after death. The two Canadian playwrights, MacDonald and Sears, can be considered more experimental in form as compared to their American colleagues, Vogel and Morrison. As the titles of their adaptations suggest, Vogel and Morrison retell the story of Desdemona with a new perspective while MacDonald and Sears dethrone Desdemona and centralize Juliet and Billie, respectively.

Rewriting a mythical figure as Shakespeare and more specifically appropriating one of his most adaptive works, is inevitably a challenging process for a new generation writer. Contemporary writers often manifest an "obvious choice" both to start "a debate with the canon" and address a wide group of readers, through Shakespeare. (Sanders 4) Especially contemporary women writers' dialogue with Shakespeare very much reflects a dialogue with what Shakespeare signifies, which obviously surpasses his personal status as William Shakespeare. As Gayle Austin reads into the process of responding to canon in dramatic form from a feminist perspective, she uses the terms "working within the canon" (which Austin identifies with liberal feminism), "expanding the canon" (which she associates with radical feminism) and "exploding the canon" (which stands for materialist feminism). (17–18) Drawing on Austin's feminist classification, it is possible to locate the four feminist adaptations in the second and third categories of political stance, namely reversal and subversion.

However, in assessing the contemporary writer's level and intention of an intertextual dialogue with an Elizabethan or Jacobean playwright, still the only one to be called 'the Great Bard', psychoanalytical perspectives on the issue of canonization cannot be undermined. Bruno Bettelheim's celebrated work *Freud and Man's Soul* provides in-depth psychoanalytical readings of both *Oedipus* and *Hamlet,* tracing their paternal relations to signs of both rivalry and admiration while also highlighting the inevitability of this process which takes place on a subconscious level. (10–30) That the two protagonists cannot escape from the destined cycle, resembles the restrictions of contemporary playwrights in responding to Shakespeare. In Harold Bloom's later psychoanalytical reading, "The largest truth of literary influence is that it is an irresistible anxiety. Shakespeare will never allow you to bury him, or escape him, or replace him. We have almost all of us, thoroughly internalized the power of Shakespeare's plays, frequently without having attended them or read them." (xviii) Building on Bloom, one can consider Shakespeare an ever 'precursor' and suggest that in an Oedipal pattern, any contemporary writer is doomed to end up repeating him while yearning for a challenge. Given the context of adapting Shakespeare, it is possibly the easiest way to start a literary battle with Shakespeare for many new generation writers whom Bloom would call 'ephebe', stuck under the heavy anxiety of Shakespearean influence. "Resenters of canonical literature are nothing more or less than deniers of Shakespeare. They are not social revolutionaries or even social rebels. They are sufferers of the anxieties of Shakespeare's influence." (xix) In other words, if obsession with Shakespeare dominates over the adaptation process, the target context inevitably gets dethroned by Shakespeare.

Shakespeare, too, is an adaptor and he has always built on the preceding texts motivated not by any challenge to the earlier writers but possibly by a search for becoming a part of the existing tradition. In her celebrated work entitled *A Theory on Adaptations*, Linda Hutcheon suggests that "adaptations of Shakespeare, in particular, intend to offer either tributes or a way to supplant canonical cultural authority." (93) It is possible to read the other three adaptations of Shakespeare under the second category of "supplant[ing] a canonical cultural authority." Toni Morrison differs from her contemporaries in adopting an adaptive strategy closer to that of Shakespeare, which both builds and signifies on the source text.

Vogel's dialogue with Shakespeare implies a feminist reversal, which as compared to MacDonald and Sears's adaptations, is more loyal in content and less subversive in form. The multiple times Pulitzer Prize winning Morrison's adaptation of Shakespeare, comparatively, reflects the least of tension. A significant reason for Morrison's distinctive authorial dialogue with the Great Bard might be that Toni Morrison, exceptionally, has already become a canonical name in her life time. This would put her outside the context of an "ephebe" and situate her on a less anxious dialogue with the

Great Bard. *Desdemona*, her recently published play, provides a new literary space for Morrison in not only proving that her literary gift transcends over generic boundaries but also in acclaiming that with her authentic feminist reflections on both African cultural heritage and Western literature, she might perhaps be a contemporary female Shakespeare.

Building on Roland Barthes's former announcement of the death of the author, Toni Morrison suggests that "Writing and reading are not all that distinct for a writer" in her groundbreaking collection of essays *Playing in the Dark*. As contemporary women playwrights appropriate *Othello* into contemporary, American, Canadian, postmodern, postcolonial or feminist contexts, they not only present themselves as contemporary readers or audiences of Shakespeare but also as new writers searching for their own places within the literary canon, as signified by Othello. Therefore, their appropriations of Othello indeed incorporate either of the motivations as revisiting the play as a "tribute" or as a challenge to "the cultural figure of canonical authority" (Hutcheon 93), which in turn relocates their Othellos as half Shakespearean. Among the contemporary women adapters of Othello, Toni Morrison's difference lies in her privileged writerly status, having become an already canonical name in her lifetime. This situation takes her to another level, where she "signify[ies] on" the Shakespearean play in the same sense that Shakespeare signified on the texts preceding his writing.

Morrison's *Desdemona* can be structurally read as a loose adaptation or an "appropriation" while its political stance or adaptive strategy in responding to Shakespeare points out a literal "revision." Re-vising *Othello*, *Desdemona* transcends over the boundaries of oppression without privileging any alternative sides of the binary poles, given contexts of both feminist and postcolonial rewrites. Morrison's strategy enables to decolonize both Desdemona and Othello's oppressed bodies, responding to Shakespeare's will in writing the play centuries before counter-oppressive theories ever flourished.

Unlike those of McDonald and Sears, Morrison's dialogue with William Shakespeare is specifically directed to a dialogue with Shakespeare's *Othello*. Different than Paula Vogel's selective concern, Morrison works on the full play and chooses to write the characters in afterlife, which Shakespeare did not represent. Vogel, however, subverts Shakespeare's characterization besides changing one of the major scenes of the play, Desdemona's last scene before avenging Othello. In her review of Morrison's *Desdemona*, Katherine Steele Brokaw notes: "If Othello is about sight, Desdemona is about sound." (361) As Brokaw's words imply, Morrison's *Desdemona* is in complementary relation to Shakespeare's *Othello*. What Shakespeare personally or collectively signifies is left out of Morrison's work, which in turn enables her *Desdemona* to reach and share *Othello*'s aura. In its relationship with the source text, Desdemona's adaptive process, comparatively, takes place on a more mature and constructive level where the adaptor subverts the source text not to oppose it by reversing its context but rather to cooperate with the source text writer by refilling the gaps in the text. In other words, Morrison's dialogue with the Great Bard is distinctive in the sense that she goes beyond the anxiety of Shakespearean influence and collaborates with him towards evoking a contemporary catharsis. Morrison's adaptation, therefore, cannot be considered as an "appropriation" as it does not intend to take the text "away from the source text." (Sanders 27) It can, however, be viewed as a feminist "revision," "writing [the female presence] back into history" (Rich 35), drawing on the effective power of subversion rather than reversal.

Quoting Adrienne Rich's words, women playwrights examined in this study commonly yearn for a "re-vision" through the instrumental space *Othello* provides. (18) However, since, drawing on Rich, this study reads "re-vision" as reconstruction or the next stage after deconstruction, the revising text is defined as one going beyond an anxious debate with the source text and adding to the source text, filling in its gaps. In this respect, Toni Morrison's *Desdemona* ends up having revised the Shakespearean tragedy while Vogel's, MacDonald's and Sears, still caught in different layers of anxiety of Shakespearean influence, have appropriated *Othello*.

The idea of canonization and recognition within academy is usually related to the search for authorial power, especially because a dialogue with Shakespeare would inevitably provide a more convenient path for any new generation writer in a search for authority. In a comparative analysis between the four contemporary women dramatists' adaptive strategies and levels of intertextual dialogues with the Great Bard, it is observed that the closer the writer is to become a canonical figure herself, the less anxious her dialogue with *Othello* gets.

This study also notes that in dramatizing patriarchy and colonialism by representing misogynistic and racist stereotypes in a well-crafted plot, Shakespeare's *Othello* accommodates any possible feminist or postcolonial rewrite. The story of *Othello* continuously inspires many projects which stand against any idea of stereotyping. In contemporary theater, *Othello* has nearly become a signifier of "revision," still providing a perpetual adaptive space for other contemporary playwrights and directors, calling them to continuously revise the text by re-representing its inspiring characters or relocating them altogether into newly discovered contexts. In their ground-breaking study, *Adaptations of Shakespeare*, Daniel Fischlin and Mark Fortier suggest "adapters of Shakespeare somehow reinforce Shakespeare's position in the canon; however it is a different Shakespeare at work." (6) This may be an ever-transforming Shakespeare, an image travelling as far as its reception can get. To put it in J. Hillis Miller's words, "There is not any 'Shakespeare' himself. 'Shakespeare' is an effect of the text, which depersonalizes, disunifies" (59), and, therefore, continuously signifies the rewriting process itself.

The comparative analyses of the four contemporary adaptations show that the less studied Canadian writers Ann-Marie MacDonald and Djanet Sears's adaptations of *Othello* get more loose in their dialogues with the source text, *Othello* and offer a more revolutionary stance in their forms of postmodern parody and black cultural appropriation, respectively. As for the Pulitzer-Prize winning American writers and professors Vogel and Morrison, who, respectively, write a prequel and a postquel to Shakespeare's *Othello*, their writerly dialogue with the Bard is observed to have situated on a less tense and more constructive level, where the writers focus on *Othello* itself by not addressing Shakespeare.

Besides her lesbian feminist perspective, Vogel differs from Morrison by foregrounding a certain part of Shakespeare's *Othello* and specifying her *Desdemona* only in relation to handkerchief, as announced in the title. In this respect, despite for different reasons, Vogel's adaptive strategy signals an appropriation of *Othello* by leaving more than one-fourth of the play untouched. Although Morrison's *Desdemona* represents the characters in an afterlife, it provides background references making the readers/audiences feel that her play adds to the Shakespearean text. Acting as both a contemporary and a canonical writer, Morrison, distinctively, cooperates with Shakespeare to fill in the gaps *Othello* introduces to her readers' or audiences' contemporary consciousness.

Borrowing the method of revising mythical sources from Shakespeare himself, new *Othello*s by contemporary women playwrights, studied in this study, reassert the "myth of Shakespeare," quoting Graham Holderness's title, or "the virtual Shakespeare" in Fischlin and Fortier's words (16). To put it in other words, despite different adaptive strategies and varying degrees of authorial dialogues, these four contemporary productions of *Othello* commonly build on the legendary presence of *Othello* in the canon, reminding the collective principle that "myths never die; they just transform." Desdemona's handkerchief, Othello's dark skin or the ladies' chamber and the Willow's song are only among the many possible signs *Othello* provides for its potential dramaturgies.

Drawing on the contemporary perspectives discussed, *Othello* can be viewed as a metatext continuously transformable as well as perpetually adaptive, especially given the context of contemporary women's drama. While Ann-Marie MacDonald and Djanet Sears foreground revolutionary feminist contexts and provide third wave feminist adaptations of *Othello*, Paula Vogel and Toni Morrison introduce comparatively closer readings of Shakespeare's play in asserting their second wave and post-feminist perspectives, respectively. Drawing on earlier discussions of Julie Sanders's understanding of "appropriation" and Adrienne Rich's conception of "revision," this study considers *Good Night Desdemona, Good Morning Juliet* and *Harlem Duet*, as feminist appropriations, while it reads *Desdemona* as a feminist revision.

The anxiety of canonization that the contemporary women playwrights experience is also addressed as an issue parallel to their authorial relations with Shakespeare. This study suggests that, although MacDonald and Sears's dialogues with the Great Bard reveal more tension and Vogel and Morrison's dialogues imply more admiration, the four contemporary adaptations of *Othello* inevitably end up in reauthorizing Shakespeare and recentering his *Othello*. In the hands of contemporary women playwrights, *Othello* thematically makes a call for new contemporary women's perspectives and technically provides an everlasting space for further feminist adaptations, already becoming a signifier of the signification process itself.

This study contends that it owns an innovative perspective both by studying these four contemporary female *Othellos* in one volume for the first time and by providing discussions on interdisciplinary and intercultural receptions of the perpetually adaptive text, *Othello*, in contemporary times. It looks forward to inspiring more contemporary women writers to work on *Othello* on the one hand and contributing to recent theoretical studies on adaptations of Shakespeare on the other.

Bibliography

Al-Dabbagh. *Shakespeare, Orient and the Critics*. New York, Washington D.C. and Berlin: Peter Lang, 2010.

Anzaldua, Gloria. *Borderlands. La Frontera. The New Mestiza*. San Francisco: Aunt Lute Books, 1999 (1987).

Aristotle. "Poetics". *Aristotle's Poetics*. Ed. O.B. Hardison. Trans. Leon Golden. Eaglewood Cliff, NJ: Prentice- Hall, 1968.

Austin, Gayle. *Feminist Theories for Dramatic Criticism*. Michigan: U of Michigan P, 2006. (1991).

Barthes, Roland. "The Death of the Author". *Image, Music, Text/Roland Barthes; essays selected and translated by Stephen Heath*. New York: Hill & Wang, 1978.

–. *The Rustle of Language*. Berkeley: U of California P, 1989.

–. *S/Z*. Trans. Richard Miller. New York: Hill and Wang: The Noonday P, 1974.

Bassnet-McGuire, Susan. *Translation Studies*. London: Methuen, 1980.

Bettelheim, Bruno. *Freud and Man's Soul*. London: Chatto & Windus, 1983.

Bhabha, Homi K. *The Location of Culture*. London and New York: Routledge, 1994.

Bloom, Harold. *The Anxiety of Influence: A Theory of Poetry*. New York: Oxford UP, 1997.

Bristol, Michael D. *Shakespeare's America, America's Shakespeare*. London: Routledge, 1990.

Brokaw, Katherine Steele. "Review of Morrison's Desdemona". *Shakespeare Bulletin*. 30.3, Fall 2012. p. 361–365.

Buntin, Mat. "Interview with Djanet Sears". March 2004. *www.canadianshakespeares.ca/i_dsears.cfm*. 10.10.2016. (web)

Cartmell, Deborah and Imelda Whelehan. *Screen Adaptation. Impure Cinema*. London and New York: Palgrave MacMillan, 2010.

Case, Sue-Ellen. "Introduction". *Performing Feminisms: Feminist Critical Theory and Theatre. Ed. Sue-Ellen Case*. Baltimore and London: The John Hopkins UP, 1990.

Chakravarti, Paromita. "Modernity, Postcoloniality and Othello: The Case of *Saptapadi*". *Remaking Shakespeare. Performance Across Media, Genres and Cultures*. Eds. P. Aebischer, E. Esche and N. Wheale. Basingstoke and New York: Palgrave-MacMillan, 2003.

Cinthio (Giovanni Battista Giraldi). *Un Capitano Moro*. (1565). Trans. J.E. Taylor. (1855) *http://www.shakespeare-navigators.com/othello/Osource. html*. 13.03.2015. (web)

Davies, Carol Boyce. *Black Women, Writing, and Identity: Migrations of the Subject*. London and New York: Routledge, 1994.

Dobson, Michael. *The Making of the National Poet Shakespeare. Adaptation and Authorship*. 1660–1769. Oxford: Oxford UP, 1992.

Du Bois, W.E.B. *The Souls of Black Folk: Essays and Sketches*. Greenwich, Conn.: Fawcett, 1961.

Eagleton, Mary and Emma Parker (Ed). *The History of British Women's Writing, 1970-Present*. London: Palgrave MacMillan, 2015.

Erickson, Peter. *Rewriting Shakespeare, Rewriting Ourselves*. California: U of California P, 1994.

Faludi, Susan. *Backlash: The Undeclared War Against American Women*. New York: Crown P, 1991.

Fischer-Lichte, Erica. *The Semiotics of Theatre*. Bloomington: Indiana UP, 1992.

Fischlin, Daniel and Mark Fortier. "Introduction". *Adaptations of Shakespeare*. Eds. Daniel Fischin and Mark Fortier. New York: Routledge, 2000.

Fortier, Mark. "Undead and Unsafe: Adapting Shakespeare in Canada". *Shakespeare in Canada*. Eds. Diana Brydon and Irena R. Makaryk. Toronto and Buffalo: U of Toronto P, 2002.

Friedman, Sharon. "The Feminist Playwright as Critic: Paula Vogel, Ann-Marie MacDonald, and Djanet Sears Interpret *Othello*". *Feminist Theatrical Revisions of Classic Works*. Ed. Sharon Friedman. Jefferson, North Carolina and London: McFarland and Company, 2009.

Gates, Henri Louis. *The Signifying Monkey: A Theory of Afro-American Literary Criticism*. New York and Oxford: Oxford UP, 1988.

Holderness, Graham (Ed). *The Shakespeare Myth*. Manchester and New York: Manchester UP, 1988.

hooks, bell. *Feminist Theory: From Margin to Center*. London: Pluto P, 2000.

Howard, Jean E. and Marion F. O'Connor. "Introduction". *Shakespeare Reproduced: The Text in History and Ideology*. Eds. Jean E. Howard and Marion F. O'Connor. New York and London: Methuen, 1987.

Hutcheon, Linda. *A Theory of Parody: The Teachings of Twentieth-Century Art Forms*. Champaign and Urbana: U of Illinois P, 2001.

Hutcheon, Linda. *A Theory of Adaptations*. New York: Routledge, 2006.

Karantay, Suat. "Çevrilmemiş yapıtlara önsözler'e bir önsöz". *Metis Çeviri*. 20.21, 1992. 111–114.

Knowles, Ric. "Othello in Three Times". *Shakespeare in Canada*. Eds. Diana Brydon and Irena R. Makaryk. Toronto and Buffalo: U of Toronto P, 2002.

–. *Shakespeare and Canada. Essays on Production, Translation and Adaptation*. Brussels: Peter Lang, 2004.

Kristeva, Julia. *Desire in Language: A Semiotic Approach to Literature and Art*. Ed. Leon S. Roudiez. Trans. Thomas Gora. New York: Columbia UP, 1980.

Lefevere, Andre. *Translation, Rewriting and the Manipulation of Literary Fame*. London and New York: Routledge, 1992.

Loomba, Ania. *Shakespeare, Race and Colonialism*. Oxford, New York: Oxford UP, 2002.

Loomba, Ania and Martin Orkin (Ed). *Post-colonial Shakespeares*. London and New York: Routledge, 1998.

MacDonald, Ann-Marie. *Goodnight Desdemona (Good Morning Juliet)*. New York: Grove P, 1988.

Miller, J. Hillis. "Ariachne's Broken Woof". *The* Georgia *Review*. 33. 1979. p. 44–60.

Moraga, Cherrie and Gloria Anzaldua. *This Bridge Called My Back: Writings by Radical Women of Color*. Berkeley: Third Woman P, 1984.

Morrison, Toni. *Playing in the Dark: Whiteness and the Literary Imagination*. London: Picador, 1993 (1992).

–. *Desdemona*. (lyrics by Rokia Traoré; with a foreword by Peter Sellars). London: Oberon Books, 2012.

–. "Recitatif". *Norton Anthology of American Literature*. Ed. Nina Baym. New York: Norton, 1995.

Newman, Karen. "And Wash the Ethiop White: Femininity and the Monstrous in Othello." "Introduction". *Cross-Cultural Performances. Differences in Women's Re-Visions of Shakespeare*. Ed. Novy, Marianne. Urbana: U of Illinois P, 1993.

Novy, Marianne. *Transforming Shakespeare. Contemporary Women's Re-visions in Literature and Performance*. Ed. Marianne Novy. New York and Hampshire: Palgrave, 1999.

Pavis, Patrice. *Languages of the Stage: Essays in the Semiology of the Theatre*. New York: Performing Arts Journal Publications, 1993.

Rhys, Jean. *Wide Sargasso Sea*. Ed. Judith L. Raiskin. New York: W.W. Norton, 1999.

Rich, Adrienne. "When We Dead Awaken: Writing as Revision". College English. 34.1, 1972: 18–30.

Said, Edward. *Orientalism*. New York: Vintage P, 1994.

Sanders, Julie. *Novel Shakespeares. Twentieth-Century Women Novelists and Appropriation*. Mancester UP, 2001.

–. *Adaptation and Appropriation*. London and New York: Routledge, 2006.

Sartre, Jean Paul. *Existentialism Is a Humanism*. Yale UP, 2007.

Sears, Djaneti. "Harlem Duet". *Adaptations of Shakespeare*. Eds. Daniel Fischin and Mark Fortier. New York: Routledge, 2000.

Sellars, Peter. "Foreword". *Desdemona*. Ed. Toni Morrison. London: Oberon Books, 2012.

Shakespeare, William. "Tragedies". *The Tragedy of Othello, The Moor of Venice*. London: Marshall Cavendish, 1988.

Showalter, Elaine. *A Literature of Their Own: British Woman Novelists from Bronte to Lessing*. London: Virago, 1999.

Silverstone, Catherine. "Othello's Travels in New Zealand: Shakespeare, Race and National Identity". *Remaking Shakespeare. Performance Across Media, Genres and Cultures*. Eds. P. Aebischer, E. Esche and N. Wheale. Basingstoke and New York: Palgrave-MacMillan, 2003.

Smith, Barbara. *Writings on Race, Gender and Freedom: The Truth that Never Hurts*. New Jersey: Rutgers UP, 1998.

Spivak, Gayatri C. "Can the Subaltern Speak". *Colonial Discourse and Postcolonial Theory. A Reader.* Eds. Patrick Williams and Laura Chrisman. New York: Columbia UP, 1994.

Sözalan, Özden. *The Staged Encounter: Contemporary Feminism and Women's Drama.* Stuttgart: Ibidem P, 2007.

Şen, Hasine. *The Power of Silence.* Sofia: *Paradox P, 2017.*

Tekinay, Aslı. "Othello Rewritten: Paula Vogel's *Desdemona*: A Play About a Handkerchief and Djanet Sears's Harlem Duet". *Tribute to Professor Oya Başak: [Re]reading Shakespeare in Text and Performance. Selected Papers from the Oya Başak Conference* [May 12–14, 2004]. Ed. Aslı Tekinay. İstanbul: Boğaziçi UP, 2005.

Truth, Sojourner. "Ain't I a Woman?". (1851). *https://sourcebooks.fordham.edu/mod/sojtruth-woman.asp.* 16.09.2016. (web)

Vaughan, Virginia M. *Othello: A Contextual History.* Oxford: Oxford UP, 1994.

Vogel, Paula. "Desdemona: A Play About a Handkerchief". *Adaptations of Shakespeare.* Eds. Daniel Fischin and Mark Fortier. New York: Routledge, 2000.

Yücel, Can. *Hamlet.* İstanbul: Papirüs Yayınları, 1998.

www.ingramcontent.com/pod-product-compliance
Lightning Source LLC
Chambersburg PA
CBHW030248100426
42812CB00002B/365